Lactating at Cats

Lactating at Cats

An Irreverent Breast Cancer Memoir with a Splash of Blood

Kate Pamp

Lactating at Cats An Irreverent Breast Cancer Memoir with a Splash of Blood.

Copyright © 2025 Kate Pamp. All rights reserved. No portion of this book may be reproduced, copied, distributed or adapted in any way, with the exception of certain activities permitted by applicable copyright laws, such as brief quotations in the context of a review or academic work.

Cover image: iStock/ArtMood Visualz

www.lactatingatcats.com

ISBN 979-8-284-27884-0

Dedication

Dedicated to you – whoever you are, and wherever you are in your chapter of your life.

You, like me might be struggling with so many more things than people around you are aware of – and sometimes it just is hard. You're not on your own.

Sometimes it feels like everyone has so much support and brilliant mates and you don't, but I think a lot of us are struggling with this a lot more than we let on. If your supporters are a bit pants, then I hope you have some wonderful pet-family to keep you going – they can be more reliable if I'm honest.

To all the people who have written their own cancer memoirs, thank you – I read lots of them and I salute you for braving it and sharing your stories. I can now relate to how much thought and work you put in – and I thank you for paving the way for mine. I'm still learning – but this one was good fun to write and you all inspired me.

To all the doctors, porters, nurses, health care assistants, the tea ladies and cleaners, OT's, physio's and radiographers who have looked after me during my three stays in hospital, I have moaned about some things but overall, I can't begin to tell you how grateful I am for the care I received. It was often the cleaners who had the brightest smile – and post-surgery I felt like crap – so I am telling you to keep going, keep smiling – it is noticed, and it is very much appreciated. x

To my fantastic writing mentor, you are a legend, you make me laugh, and I'm so grateful for you helping me get going with this book. You are a mine of knowledge and I can't thank you enough for your generosity of time x.

To my gorgeous high calibre top class small but perfectly curated friends – you know who you are. I apologise for being weird and being there one minute and then disappear for months because I get overwhelmed. I'm sorry to those of you who offered to come and stay but I couldn't say yes because I was embarrassed my house was a bit messy and I didn't have the energy to fix it. I couldn't be sure I had the energy to cook for you, or take you anywhere nice, and I was worried if you did stay you would see me struggling and worry, and then I would feel sad and that would knock my confidence.

To my two friends who made the long journey and met me out somewhere – I can't thank you enough – you are far more than friends – you are family to me, and no matter what life throws at you I will be here for you to repay your kindness, no matter what.

To my amazing, fantastic husband – wow did I bag a good one, I had to go through quite a few duds before finding this one and it was totally worth the wait. He has had my back and championed me from the get-go, whereas some of my previous partners I know – would have either left the minute the poop hit the fan, or made my life an absolute misery had they stayed.

My husband is the best listener, he is kind, he sticks up for me, he believes in me, and best of all I love every single thing about him including his weird taste in music, the fact he makes me watch videos about double slit experiments, how people spoke in the 14th Century, how to approach breaking up a 130 tonne fatberg in the London sewers and time lapsed decomposing vegetables. His exotic eyes and weird food combinations and his pert bum – he is the best father our children could have and I thank everything that I ever found him.

To my beautiful children, I wanted to be a young mum but it took me ages for me to wade through idiot boyfriends and eventually I found your dad and we made you – you are both amazing – I'm so proud of how clever and beautiful you both are – I can't believe my luck, and come hell or high water am I giving up any battle and missing out on you growing up. I can't thank you both enough for all your patience hanging around hospital waiting rooms, eating crap food at the hospital canteen – and having to put up with mummy being in a bit of a state at the best of times. Cancer pooped on some of your best years and I'm going to do my best to try to make it up to you. xxx

Finally, to Doris, thank you. You entered my life just when I needed you. I hope you are having fun with your lovely husband and cats, that you are comfy and are having all of your favourite treats – I'm sending you a massive hug, and look forward to a jolly good natter at some point. xxx

Contents

Note To Reader

Chapter 1	'Pain Is Not A Symptom of Breast Cancer'	1
Chapter 2	The News Sinks In	13
Chapter 3	How Did My Children Take It?	17
Chapter 4	Mental Diarrhoea	21
Chapter 5	Talking To Other People About My Diagnosis	25
Chapter 6	What Caused My Cancer?	27
Chapter 7	Snake Oil & Insanity Purchases	29
Chapter 8	Eviction Nightmare	33
Chapter 9	The Booby Show & Tell	35
Chapter 10	Summary Of Plan From This Point	43
Chapter 11	The First Surgery	45

Chapter 12	Post Surgery Euphoria!	51
Chapter 13	Moving House	61
Chapter 14	The Results	67
Chapter 15	The Recovery	71
Chapter 16	Final Decision To Go Boobless	73
Chapter 17	Doris	81
Chapter 18	Managing Information	85
Chapter 19	Keeping Going	89
Chapter 20	The Crap Advice	93
Chapter 21	A Dabble With Religion	99
Chapter 22	Clinical Psychology	103
Chapter 23	Enter – The Abyss	105
Chapter 24	Second Surgery – The Double Mastectomy	109
Chapter 25	Post Surgery Recovery	115
Chapter 26	Further Surgery Issues	117
Chapter 27	Lovely Doris	125
Chapter 28	The Pregnant Pigeon	129
Chapter 29	Investigations	131
Chapter 30	Aromatase Inhibitors	133

Chapter 31	Doctor Google	143
Chapter 32	An Obsession With Time	149
Chapter 33	My Confidence Took A Hit	151
Chapter 34	I Thought I Was Supposed To Get Thin	153
Chapter 35	Experimenting With What To Wear	155
Chapter 36	Other People's Perceptions – Feeling Invisible	159
Chapter 37	Competition Of Who's Had The Worst Health Problems	163
Chapter 38	Who Is For You? Who Is Against You?	165
Chapter 39	Who Did I Let Go Of And Who Did I Gather Up For The Journey Onwards?	167
Chapter 40	Listening To Others' Problems In The Early Days Can Be Hard	171
Chapter 41	Sex Life	173
Chapter 42	Operation Number Three	175
Chapter 43	Post Surgery Number Three	185
Chapter 44	Phoenix Rising (Hopefully)	189
Chapter 45	Tips To Manage Aromatase Inhibitors	191
Chapter 46	Write Your Meds Down	197

Chapter 47	Would I Recommend Flat Closure Mastectomy?	201
Chapter 48	Managing Who You Tell What	205
Chapter 49	Things I'd rather people didn't say to me…	211
Chapter 50	Other Tips	215
Chapter 51	Final Thoughts	259
Chapter 52	Final Message To Reader	279
P.S.		285

Note To Reader

I am a car crash of a person at the best of times – so when cancer rocked up a few years ago it was quite the fiasco.

At that time, I struggled to find a book to read that focused on not just the cancer itself, but the mental health aspects of the aftermath too, in particular health anxiety.

What happens if you are diagnosed with cancer on top of living with other mental health issues?

Much as the cancer has been a story about physical health, it *annihilated* my mental health, I had already been living with a diagnosis of OCD and bipolar disorder for many years.

This is my personal account of how cancer hit my mental health, how I fought to manage my mental health like a boss *in spite of* cancer and ends with some final thoughts to the reader about things I learned along the way just in case any of them help you.

This is not so much a book discussing the clinical ins and outs of how cancer itself, it's more about the back end of the show long past the bit when people are bored poop-less of hearing about your cancer journey and believe me, they will be.

This book is not about recommending flat closure mastectomy – in a nutshell <u>I do not recommend this surgery at all</u>.

I don't regret having this surgery, I am actually very pleased with my results – but I'm trying to do the responsible thing and not sugar-coat how major this surgery is, both mentally and physically. It was the right surgery for me, and it might be for you, it's just that I'm writing from the perspective that it is obviously *purely* your decision to weigh and balance, and I'm not going to pretend that it's all 'happy flattie' in case I give ambivalent people the wrong idea.

It has been painful and grueling, and the longstanding psychological effects are real. On bad days – I'm only on the cusp of handling it myself, so I genuinely think it wouldn't be for everyone.

Reconstructive surgeries like Diep flap and LD flap, can have some magnificent results - I've seen women who have had these surgeries and some of the results were just stunning. It took quite a lot for me to turn my back on these options.

I write this book hoping to flag up issues you might not have thought about.

Ultimately, it's you who will live with the surgery you chose – with good research, hopefully you'll choose the right one for you.

One final note here – is to say that throughout the book I will detail every mental and physical symptom, this is not for the purpose of sympathy, as in my day-to-day life I don't keep banging on about it, it's more to help those of you experiencing any of these symptoms feel 100% validated.

In a life where it can *feel* like *virtually no one* around you seems to understand the trauma of cancer, and the sheer agony that aromatase inhibitors and other treatments *can* bring – I want you to know that I understand, it is for this reason that I spare no detail.

Despite all the moans laid out in this book, I was able to continue to go about my usual routine, albeit I did not drive at all at times of severe leg pain – I always waited until those symptoms had subsided – this will make sense later on.

For the record, I had:-
- Oestrogen receptive
- Stage one
- Grade two
- Breast cancer
- With no lymph node involvement

I did not need chemotherapy, or radiotherapy, so I have not written anything about those two treatments in this book.

This book is really a book in parts, one part is about the fallout of discovering I had cancer, another is a huge moan about the hell of aromatase inhibitors, then I tell you how living with this crap changed my outlook on people, and then there's a variety of self-management stuff, a lot of it I've picked up online in breast cancer groups that helped me, that I've shared with you in case any of them are good for you too. I've bared all about my own health anxiety too.

I'm assuming you'll take any of my book with a pinch of salt – we are all so different, and you know yourself better than anyone – I'm sure you're make your own mind up about which bits are helpful to you and just bin off the rest.

Anywhere I mention <u>pre-loading</u> – I'm talking about taking painkillers before a procedure, not alcohol!

Once I had written everything I'd wanted to say, I made no attempt to fatten the book up unnecessarily – so it might not be as long as some other books – but I hope there's not too much stating the obvious kind of stuff in here either as I personally find that very annoying.

That gorgeous woman on the front cover <u>is not</u> me! – Wow, I wish it was.

I chose her for the book cover as she puts me in mind of *how I feel like I am on the inside* – an edgy cool woman surrounded by cats. I was young in the 1980's and love that big hair and sassy vibe she has going on there.

Not saying I'm the best-looking woman in the world, but breast cancer did many things, including stealing any looks that I had left in my forties. (I hope to work on self-care in time).

This will make more sense as you go along through the book, but for reference – I'm the tired looking pudgy short dumpling browsing granny pants at the supermarket – and despite my round size – I'm mostly invisible – a shadow of my former self and I blend into the background like the palest of wallflowers.

What I am hanging onto with all my might however – is my sense of humour, which keeps me going through the toughest of times, I hope yours does too. x

Who is this book written for?
People who are considering whether to go for flat closure mastectomy.

People who are planning to have breast reconstruction like Diep flap, LD or implants and want reassurance they are doing the right thing, might get something out of this book.

People who feel alone with their nightmare with aromatase inhibitors might appreciate the validation regarding the plethora of hideous side effects. (If you're on aromatase inhibitors and not getting side effects then you might feel quite relieved given what I experienced).

People who experienced the interpersonal issues and cancer-ghosting post-*any cancer* or had rude awakenings re *how rubbish people can be post-cancer* might appreciate the latter part of the book.

People who are just curious from the outside might find it interesting I guess – maybe the final thoughts and takeaways might have some benefit for them too.

I will say the obvious here – which is – please don't take anything I say as medical advice – as you read on, you will clearly realise that this is not a text book.

This book is not written using artificial intelligence, in fact it's written with very little intelligence at all. I wrote this book in the plainest language as possible, avoided being unnecessarily fancy and just generally written it the way I speak – hence it isn't going to read as perfect English – whatever that is.

I guess I ought to give a bit of a trigger warning, the book is somewhat unfiltered, parts of my book lean towards the graphic – I don't sugar coat the fact that one surgery was agony – (albeit not for long at all), there's a bit of crudity in places, I blame myself for my own cancer quite a bit, I mention narcissistic and mean people, and I say the word 'crap' too much.

I have, however, dug deep into the depths of my soul to share with you a very personal story of how cancer affected me. Every time I had thoughts that were embarrassing, selfish or just bizarre, I jotted them down and put them in here. Quite a weird thing to do and this could go horribly wrong, and for this reason, some inconsequential details have been changed to protect privacy.

This memoir was written with tears, laughter and post mastectomy an actual splash of blood.

Kate x

Chapter 1
'Pain Is Not A Symptom of Breast Cancer'

Bollocks.

My left boob had never quite been normal.

Now I cast my mind back, ever since the birth of my first baby – that boob had leaked occasionally at the sound of *any* random baby crying.

Come to think of it, I'm embarrassed to say that it also leaked at the sound of a hungry cat meowing – what is wrong with me!

I mean I love cats, but I definitely *did not* want to breast feed them!

This was happening long after I had stopped breastfeeding – which makes me wonder if my boobs have just always been a bit weird.

I recently watched a documentary about cat behaviour on a well-known streaming platform which talked about this very phenomenon – of cats mimicking the cry of a baby to get attention.

This wasn't something I mentioned to my doctor mind you – imagine putting that on the request form to see your GP... Problem – 'Lactating at Cats'... hmm, no thank you, so I ignored it until...

2022 and I had boob pain – sharp stabby electric shock pains in my left boob.

I'd already presented to the Emergency Department just a few months previously – to complain of this *very* pain and been checked out for heart problems and promptly discharged.

From much of the guidance for symptoms of breast cancer that I'd seen – I had learned that 'pain was not a symptom of breast cancer'. Yet here I was again with the exact same sharp pains, along with what felt like an all-over 'glowing' pain which came and went. I was convinced it was the ridiculously stiff bath tap in our rented house causing the pain, but when watching telly in bed that night, I decided to further investigate by having a feel of my boob.

I had a good fish around and was unnerved to find a lump deep inside my left boob – which I seemed to be able to nudge from left to right. It was directly under the nipple – but as deep as you can detect. I carried on watching telly, thinking the lump was *probably just another one of those cyst type things*, probably not anything at all. I mentioned it to my husband; we still thought it was most likely innocent, and we carried on as usual – watched our history programme and went to sleep.

The next day, something was niggling me and I thought I ought to contact my GP.

I was seen the same day – a lovely warm, kind GP – Dr Meadows – had a good mangling of my boob, and I expected the usual news of it most likely being that cyst or something. This time however, there was an eerier atmosphere – something a bit off. She said 'hmmm... it's probably nothing, but I think we need to get this checked out'. It wasn't so much *what she said* – but *the way she said it* which unnerved me – there was a cautious seriousness to the way she spoke – not the usual jaunty 'oh it's probably nothing' vibe. I wasn't used to GP's behaving like this, any lumps and bumps I've ever presented with before has amounted to mostly nothing. This was different.

She referred me to the 'One stop boob clinic' – the wait was up to two weeks.

I felt completely thrown after this appointment; I drove home with a spaced-out empty sinking feeling. Over the evening, my husband and I attempted again to pass it off as *probably nothing*, but this time I lay in bed with my mind racing about what the scan might show. The following ten days or so until my appointment at the clinic was a tense time, kind friends chimed in with the 'honestly it'll be just a cyst' too – eventually I believed it, so when I did attend the one stop breast clinic – it was a nasty shock.

The One Stop Boob Clinic Appointment
My husband and I went along to the clinic, we had no one to babysit the children, we'd recently moved across country to the other and had no help whatsoever. Our children

followed me along to quite a few of my breast cancer appointments like obedient little ducks.

We met the breast surgeon – Mrs. Morgan a short kind person who had reassuring kind eyes and a gentle bedside manner. Behind the curtain – the surgeon examined me, and in a moment – my whole world felt completely surreal. She stood back – hands in the air and said – 'It is suspicious'.

CRAP. Not what I wanted to hear at all.

That dark silence engulfed me again. I discovered a quiet hideousness where bad news lurks. I felt an immediate poo pain, as my body had decided quicker than I could process – that this was big enough news that I was going to need to evacuate my bowels *very* soon.

'My life is over, I'm going to die, I'm going to lose my hair, I'm going to be thin and frail on chemo, and my children – my children are going to have no mother' were all thoughts that pervaded my mind all in an instant.

I was whisked to X-Ray from which point I was pinged around the hospital like a pinball wizard machine. I had a mammogram, then pinged across to ultrasound, which turned out to be a terrifying experience. A moderately grumpy looking health care assistant got me set up on the hospital bed, the equipment ready, and the sonographer came over – who already seemed tense. She started to scan my boob whilst staring intently at the monitor. I did my usual and gabbled at her in the hope of attaining an up to the millisecond newsflash – no such luck – *'quiet please'* she said in a stressed, tense voice – and I knew again, that this was not looking good at all.

Even the health care assistant was deathly silent as he watched every move over my breast on the monitor. It's always rubbish to be last in line for the news about yourself – and being the last to find out what was going on here seemed to go on for an age. I could feel my irritable bowel kicking off again.

Finally, the sonographer stopped what she was doing, and said it looked like cancer.

'Could it be a 'cyst' or something?' I said – 'no – it is not a cyst' – she said with a finality I wasn't ready for.

I was going to need a biopsy. Damn.

Contrary to what I thought a breast biopsy would be like – it was actually okay. It was one of those things that *sounded terrible* – I mean it's your boob – it must be painful, but for me, with the pain relief on board I felt lucky that I could manage it just fine. It felt like a really deep physio massage, albeit a bit numb. Lots of excessive pushing about, like an enthusiastic baker kneading his dough, or like one of those chonky cats making biscuits – except a lot more vigorous.

If I was to rate medical procedures for hideousness – I would say easily that the boob biopsy would come in last place at number five. In at four with its unwieldly long wand – I would place the 'vaginal ultrasound'. At three is the ever scrapey smear test – particularly as my inner parts veer off to one side and they can never find my cervix. Coming in at number two – would have to be the 'colonoscopy' – I mean the build up to that is quite special, with its vile tasting drinks and pooing foam for England the night before – I'm still traumatised from ring sting to this day. And the wind created raspberry sounds out my bathroom window so loud even the crows were saying *'ooh I say'*.

Top of the list of lady torture was for me – the 'hysteroscopy' – which I mistakenly thought I could do without anesthetic. I've had children – how bad can it be I thought? How bad can it be? – it's 'Jaws up your foof' – it's a T Rex clamped to your innermost bits – what is it with the jawsy clampy thing they jam up there and start chomping off bits of your insides – is that really necessary? *'It is a bit bitey isn't it!'* said the nurse. YES – it's <u>VERY BITEY</u> and I want it to <u>stop</u>, I thought, and that was on 30mg of codeine that I'd pre-loaded before the appointment – and they didn't even tell me to do that – I just knew this was going to be a bad one.

How on earth do women manage to do this on no pain relief whatsoever? I take my hat off to them, perhaps my pain threshold is skew-wiff – but there is no way I could do a hysteroscopy cold turkey.

I'm old and now savvy enough, to know that medical letters only give you half the information you need – they don't tell you *how painful* these appointments will be. What they should actually say, is:-

'Dear (Insert name here), you have an appointment for a ………….. on ……………..
Please be aware that you may suffer agonising pain akin to that experienced by peasants in Medieval England – and no member of

staff that welcomes you/takes your weight/height/blood pressure is likely to warn you of this, due to compassion fatigue/burnout/would generally just rather be at home watching chonky cat videos on social media.

Please ensure that you take the appropriate pain relief needed to apprehend an Indian elephant, please also ensure that you don't smell on arrival as we have recently experienced a high level of patients attending appointments with poor levels of personal hygiene.

Yours faithfully
The hospital.

So, back to the biopsy – the radiographer was working so hard – her head was bright red and sweating. She was pushing and struggling like hell – but the elusive lump kept moving. I was impressed with her steely determination – she was not going to give up. After much wrangling with my mangled tit – she managed to harpoon it – twice and get two samples. Two in case the first sample was duff. Finally, she marked the cancer with a clip – so that it could be easily seen in future scans.

When she finished, she mopped her brow and looked like she'd just given birth. She was triumphant that she'd won the war with what I now discovered was a four centimeters slug shaped cancer. *'That was the hardest biopsy I've ever done'* she said. *'It kept moving, it wouldn't stay in one place,'* she said. Only I could have a 'difficult cancer' I thought. This whole one stop clinic took approximately three hours; I was mentally and emotionally drained.

My gut reaction was to drive across country to see my family, but I was poorly, well – I guess technically I thought, I was dying, and needed treatment – so I didn't go.

The following ten days were some of the worst days of my life, deathly thoughts pervaded my mind and my sleep was shocking. It had been a ten day wait for the biopsy results, given I have the patience of a toddler the wait was agonising.

The Appointment for the Boob Biopsy Results
I was called into the hospital to be given the results in person.

You know bad news is coming when the two nurses rush in to join the doctor and stand to attention ready to give you your news.

I remember being acutely aware that my life was in the Doctor's hands – I thought *'if I smile and be as polite as possible – maybe she might want to save my life even more'*.

Apparently, I had been 'lucky' and received the 'sleepy lazy cancer' which can be slow to grow.

No chemotherapy or radiotherapy *needed before the operation.*

I heard two things. 1) I need an operation – I already knew this, but it was just sinking in. 2) No chemotherapy *before* the operation. I was very confident that I would need chemotherapy after the operation and was preparing for that.

My initial response was of wanting to 'take the lot away' – <u>double mastectomy and no messing</u>. The team mentioned a couple of other surgery options which might suit me – which included a lumpectomy and a mastectomy. My gut feeling was telling me to go for the double mastectomy, I definitely did not want the lumpectomy – in all honesty – the lumpectomy may have been perfectly adequate to remove my cancer, but I knew immediately that this was not going to suit my anxious ruminating personality. I would always worry that some cancerous cells would be left behind, so it was always going to be the mastectomy for me, the issue was more about reconstruction or not.

Anyway, back to the surgeon – she gave me hope of surviving, and for this I'll be forever grateful. I'm sure it isn't for everyone – but I rather liked how my surgeon simplified all my news – she gave me the bones of what I needed to know – but didn't bang on about it. At that time – in the pure trauma of it all, I couldn't take much more in. She had a reassuring air of wisdom about her and from that point I wished I could take her home with me, I could sit her on the chair next to me just to provide reassurance when thoughts are spiraling into a vortex of ruminations – 'I will be okay won't I?' I could ask, and she could say 'yes, you're going to be absolutely fine'.

Leaving the hospital that day was eerie and surreal. I remember it like one of those flashback sequences in a film – all grey and odd. I really did feel the rug being pulled from under me. I stood outside the hospital, saw the cars continuing to drive, people chatting, and yet there I was feeling so small, not knowing how long I was going to live.

What does anyone do when they discover they have cancer?

Well, I got busy trying to do useful things that might help me over the coming months.

Everything was difficult though – as trying to do anything useful when your concentration is trashed is difficult. Plus, everywhere I went I was reminded of boobs, from the obvious cherry topped buns in shops, to everything I saw looked booby shaped – I'd never noticed it so much before, but now there were painful reminders everywhere. Even my go-to programme for relaxation about a farm kept banging on about *tits* – *sheep's tits* and loads of them.

I did a fair amount of shopping, including one of my first purchases which was an ornament of a little tortoise – which was a little reminder that 'slow and steady wins the race' which came to be my personal motto.

I bawled my eyes out in the chemist at some poor young assistant – I had learned that black nail polish might help preserve my nails when I have chemotherapy – but the minute I mentioned it to the assistant – her look of pure sympathy set me off – it was one of many moments which were just terrible. She was very understanding but it took some doing to gather myself to get out of the shop looking less than a train wreck.

Everywhere I looked – people seemed healthy, happy, and there I was dying, until I got surgery and then who knows. Who knew that I would ever experience health envy

– just wishing so much I was healthy again like everyone else.

For a while, cancer became the vegan/protein[1] shake announcement of all introductions when meeting new people – I felt utterly compelled to tell <u>everyone</u>. It was so much on the forefront of my mind that it kept spilling out everywhere. But underpinning every single thought I had was the nagging unthinkable thought that I may not be there for my two children after all – how horrific.

One of my few diary entries at this time says 'I feel a deep sadness for those who get different news' – I felt pleased *somewhat* about my hopeful news, but just so sad for those who's news isn't so good. Although for those initial weeks – deep down I had convinced myself that I was stage 4, and once I had stepped into that space it felt like a dual reality and was a feeling I would never forget to this day.

I'm just adding this bit prior to publishing…

When I was newly diagnosed – I was highly emotional and unfortunately made the mistake of forgiving certain people a whole range of cruel, low effort and quite honestly neglectful behaviours from my past, without really thinking it through. The strong emotions associated with discovering you have a life-threatening illness can really skew your judgement.

If people were mean to me *before cancer* – then they are still going to be mean to me *after cancer*, it's just that *for a*

---

[1] Nothing against vegans – I was a vegan once.

while they might hide it better. And I later discovered that when I was doing better they were nowhere to be seen.

Chapter 2
The News Sinks In

As the news sank in, I spent a good deal of time crying a lot – particularly when I saw my children. I tried to be discreet and not wail in front of them constantly, but very occasionally, the tears rolled down my cheeks uncontrollably, when I looked at them, how beautiful, how clever they were which made it more painful. The children did not deserve this at all (no children do obviously), but this was especially painful as we had just uprooted them from one side of the country to the other, this was to be a time of adventure – except it wasn't – for them it was disruptive, lots of hanging around, unsettling and very confusing.

Every day felt a repeat of the day before – I woke up feeling that moment of normality – then BOOM - the realisation that I have cancer hit and I was floored.

Some people start the day with a bit of yoga, a few affirmations – but here I was starting each day wondering if I might die soon and wondering if I could I be saved. No matter what I did – these insidious thoughts crept in and ruined just about everything. You know things are crap when you're putting the coffee in the fridge and your keys in the bin.

The only thing that did help was to keep going as best I could for my husband and children. Something I learned years ago was that when the poop hits the fan it can really help to keep up with as many of your usual routines as possible – the sudden stopping of your daily routine can worsen a crisis rather than help it, as it gives you more time to wallow in how weird your life suddenly is. At least with an *air of normality* we have a fighting chance of pretending things are okay.

My brain seemed to divide into two compartments, the outer shallow bit which could just about manage to cough out a few vaguely appropriate words when bumping into the neighbour, buying something from the shop, paying for petrol, and then my inner brain – which was OBSESSED with the cancer.

A friend would text and say, 'how are you?' – my inner brain would respond 'I'm dying – how are you?', and so this would repeat itself over and over –

it was e x h a u s t i n g.

Occasionally – the barrier between compartments got muddled and I'd start wailing at someone for simply 'asking how I was', or sobbing at my older neighbour when bringing our bins in. Occasionally random strangers were subject to being blasted my life story, which I do now feel bad for, but I had no one to talk to where we lived other than my lovely husband, and some friends on the phone – but I didn't want to trouble them too much, so I muddled through much of this alone.

There was one morning when I had congratulated myself for doing well and having a productive morning in spite of it all, I remember the postman passed me my parcel – he only asked how I was, and I just cried and cried at the doorstep – the sight of him pitying me still sticks in my mind today – I must have been quite a sorry sight. I feel bad about this now, as it must be hard for your loved ones to deal with a huge outpouring of emotions, let alone the postman – sorry postie!

I then became obsessed with warning as many people as possible about breast cancer, or any cancer for that matter. I was horrified at the breast cancer posters not stating that 'pain could be a symptom' and took it upon myself to save as many people as I could. I told everyone from the man who fixed my boiler, to the shop assistant at the haberdashery. My husband was amazed at how quickly I could get down to brass tacks with complete strangers – 'you were only there five minutes!' – he would say.

Now, looking back, it was a long time before that mission subsided. I don't mention it to many people I meet anymore, for reasons I'll go into later on, but the urge to share has all but gone, I just want to get on with my life, and I'm pretty sure people don't want to hear me trauma dumping all over the place – they have enough on their own plates as it is.

There were phone calls with my parents – but I was doing my best *not to worry them*, I was simplifying news, omitting bits, none of which was helpful to me in the end. There's not so much use in a call to family when you're so worried about *worrying them* – that the interaction becomes just a drain on your own energy, of which I had very little.

We had lived in a rented house in a beautiful town for about ten months prior to the cancer. The house itself was a tired Victorian house, but it was in a gorgeous town with beautiful buildings, a smattering of charity shops – which is one of our families' favourite hobbies aside from car boot sales.

We'd been so excited about moving to this part of the world and had been desperate to explore, but what we actually ended up using more than anything – was the darned hospitals. There were hospitals everywhere (lucky for us eh) – and we certainly did a great job of visiting all of them – a bit like a pub crawl – but a very rubbish one. If I wanted to be seen earlier – it was best to take the appointments wherever they popped up – so I saw the same surgeon all over the place, and again the poor kids trailed around like little ducks, they did very well though – I'm amazed at how resilient they seemed to be back then.

Chapter 3
How Did My Children Take It?

We had heard that some people don't tell their children they have cancer – this wasn't going to be an option for us – there was going to be a lot of hospital trips, and with no one to help, the more clued up the kids were – the less confusion. Even if we hadn't moved at all - we'd have not had any help due to distance, so we were kind of used to it.

My youngest wanted to know - 'Mummy – why do you keep getting things that might kill you?' – was one of the memorable questions. It was a good question, I'd already had sepsis post pregnancy, and this year a whole load of new health problems decided to land on me at once – could they have not just staggered themselves a bit.

Lots of people asked how my children took it – the truth is – they looked mildly dazed and oblivious. They didn't really seem to take it in very much, and my son was far more concerned about the thought of me losing my hair – that was something he was not at all happy about and he stated that very clearly. When we told the children, my only reference point was scenes from soap opera or something – I expected high drama, tears, tight hugs – maybe a family group hug, husband collapsing on the floor – sobbing loudly, banging the floor with his fists, but the reality far less dramatic.

For the children, there were way too many hospital appointments though. The journeys alone, to a variety of different hospitals, were becoming a huge pain in the arse. My daughter had mastered the art of audio description and would provide the running commentary to and from the clinics. 'Charlie is wiping his bogeys on the window', 'Charlie is smearing his dirty feet on the seats' – the journeys continued, and so did the commentary the more tired the children got. They did their best though, and by about halfway through this nightmare, they had mastered the art of being amazing, whilst sitting outside clinic rooms, in a strange place, waiting for mummy, they had sadly become resigned to it.

Eating on the hoof became the norm – although rushing from A to B with kids in tow and not wanting to miss your appointment due to roadworks led me to say nonsense like – *'you can only have your coke when you've finished your nuggets'* (not one of my finer moments), but for a short while – thank goodness for McDonalds.

Hospital food was both a blessing and a nightmare – I loved the stodgy comfort food, and really appreciated having that, as I was mentally so spent by the time we got home, but sometimes it was really hard, because the kids were understandably fractious from hanging around were impossible to tame in the queue for food.

Hospital staff looked frustrated and irritated at how long it would take for us to find something the kids would eat – I could see the irritation in their faces and thought 'if only they knew what we were going through' – but of course they didn't, and to them we were just holding them up from their miniscule lunch break.

I allowed myself a private weep in the loo every now and again, but on the whole tried to put a brave face on it for the children. I told them that mummy would *most likely* be okay, but we just had a lot of disruption for the next six months.

Little did I know that that figure would be more like five years. A note from my diary in those early days reads[2]:–

'The news has sunk in, and I feel gutted – just gutted.

The prospect of leaving my kids at their age terrifies me, I'm devastated beyond belief. My husband is amazing, but he looks exhausted, and I feel so bad at the hideous time he is having.

I feel trapped in a dark cloud. I still don't know what type or stage my cancer is, and the wait is agonizing.

I wish my husband could stay home with me all the time; I don't like being alone.

I don't mind about my hair, the mastectomy or even chemo – I just want to get rid of it. I feel terrible all day, I'm lucky to feel even just two minutes of brightness.

I was up at midnight vomiting last night – has the cancer spread or is it something I ate.

---

[2] Written when I thought I needed chemo.

The flowers and cards are making me feel like I'm at my own funeral, and virtually nothing anyone says can help'.

Chapter 4
Mental Diarrhoea

I live with a diagnosis of bipolar disorder.

I know if I'm getting a bit 'fast' – life feels beautiful and my right armpit stinks. I pop a mood stabiliser and *poof* I run at normal speed again.

I wasn't diagnosed until my forties, but as I cast my mind right back to my childhood and beyond - I could see a plethora of terrible choices I'd made on the back of mood disturbances, not to mention the dual diagnosis of self-medicating with alcohol – when the penny dropped I was gutted, many a trail of destruction had already happened and the regret over that was something I was going to have to live with.

Nowadays, on the lowest of doses I'm kept ticking over quite nicely like a vintage car – no major issues. I just wish I'd known in my twenties as just a few crumbs of these meds could have prevented me from getting myself into unsafe situations. My past history is punctuated by a catalogue of risky decisions, whereas post-mood stabiliser I'm rather a boring old fart. Drama is seriously not my thing, so I'm taking the boring old fart thing and running with it.

My idea of exciting these days is rummaging for treasure at a car boot sale or watching nature programmes – how things change.

But I do also live with OCD, and fluctuating anxiety that can be completely disabling. So, when I'm stressed I do still gabble. It's a clear sign that I'm doing my best to make sense of a rollercoaster of horrific-ness occurring in my mind – but it does impact people around me and for this reason, I can be all or nothing person – people either cross the road to avoid me or pull up a chair and lean in.

How cancer affected my OCD – well – I had gone from usual circumstances of checking the front door was locked twice, to checking it ten times. The other OCD symptom was to check my handbrake was on in a *particularly weird way,* carefully putting it on and off <u>three times</u> until my brain said it was *fine* – to post-cancer diagnosis - yanking it up so high – that one of these days it'll come clean out of its socket – like a caveman with a bone ripped from an animal with all its bloody sinews dangling. I imagined holding the handbrake triumphantly – yes! – I'd finally overpowered it – except I hadn't – I'd just broken the car and would have to explain my mental-ness it to the garage man.

Having additional medication to take *as well* as cancer meds though is a monumental nuisance. My bipolar meds are very disheartening because they make me tired in the mornings and give me a sudden appetite the minute they kick in at bedtime – which has far too often led me on a midnight quest to find the biscuit tin.

It just felt very unfair that not only was I having to manage this cancer rubbish, but I had other mental health crap that I was already managing as well, and the cocktail of meds I was on were all interacting in annoying ways.

Weight gain is a real nuisance.

My tummy sticks out so much it operates the washing machine without me knowing it. Part of the reason for this is because of my mood stabiliser which makes me so hungry I could practically lift up the entire fridge and tip it down my throat.

I have proved this so many times, as I can be 'not hungry all day' then forty-five minutes after taking it I am ravenous. These meds need to be taken at bedtime because they make me tired, but that then means midnight waking = midnight snacks. It doesn't sound like much, but when you have an oestrogen receptive cancer, it hangs out in your fat cells – so the whole point is to reduce those fat cells if you can, and my midnight snacking has and still is an uphill battle, it really is a fight to live.

Try telling my subconscious mind that it's inadvisable to eat at midnight and it just covers its ears and shouts la la la. Those meds affect my appetite and clearly affect my decision making – it's like I turn into someone who is completely unable to comprehend logic in the middle of the night. If I can get through one night having woken hungry and not snacked – it's a triumph.

Chapter 5
Talking To Other People About My Diagnosis

There were quite a few times when other people wanted to hear all about the nitty gritty of my cancer, but sometimes it was the last thing I wanted to think about.

I ended up having some bizarre conversations where I was being grilled by people I didn't know *that well* about the stages of my cancer so much, one neighbour gave me a pumping migraine.

Sometimes I wanted to talk about it, sometimes I didn't. At times – I worked so hard to try to bring the conversation around to something positive – like a beach we wanted to visit, or the kids, or anything but the darn cancer, but you can't – when people want to go there they're like a dog with a bone – 'oh alright then let's talk about my cancer, let's get right into it, dig deep until I feel utterly drained for the rest of the day then we can all go home. It will take me a day to recover at least but what the heck'.

People's responses can also vary from – 'I'd rather chew gravel' than hear about your cancer journey – to and

FBI level interrogation. If faced with said FBI level interrogation – feel free find some way of saying 'no comment' – this is something I wish I'd thought about earlier on was that just because someone asks you something doesn't mean to say you have to answer it, often its casual acquaintances doing this.

Fortunately, I could rely on my inner circle of mates who were able to be present in just the way I needed – there weren't many of them, but I am very grateful for them and the support they kindly gave me. They were however all busy people with jobs and kids, and I didn't like to put on them too much, so there were a lot of times I just muddled along without bothering them too much.

Chapter 6

What Caused My Cancer?

The number one suspect was the cigarettes that I smoked for sixteen years – wow do I regret that now, I've also inhaled a huge amount of passive smoke in my lifetime, that can't have been good either.

Next in line was the alcohol I enjoyed over many decades in varying amounts – I grew up in the age of the binge – a tipple didn't exist in my social groups – if you went out you got hammered and that was that.

In the 2000's I used way too much anti-bacterial spray and other cleaning products. I now try to avoid using chemicals as much as possible now, and if I do use it, I wear gloves – better late than never.

My mind churns over all the things I do that *might not be great for my health* – how about when I open the dishwasher door before it's finished and end up getting a dishwasher tab facial sauna – it honestly can't be great.

Maybe it's all the ultra-processed food I've eaten – I was obsessed with instant snack noodles in the 1980's, and radioactive looking pop – so many culprits – maybe it was a combination of it all.

If I serve up bad food to my family now, I feel intense shame – yet it's so hard, for reasons I'll go into later on, as the whole cancer journey leaves me at times *utterly exhausted* – a tiredness I've never experienced before which makes it feel impossible to stay standing by teatime, let alone rustle up healthy home cooked fayre and then clear it all up.

Maybe it was stress – I've had a lot of that, and one of the main problems and still is, is my chronic hypervigilance – which creates a living nightmare of being able to spot people who are being mean within seconds. It's like living in some kind of dual reality – I can't tolerate behaviour that others seem to find completely acceptable, and at times it makes me feel like I'm going a bit mad. I wish at times that I was thick to mean-ness, then I wouldn't have to go about avoiding people and getting myself into and out of awkward situations.

My husband is kind, and always saying that the cancer was most likely not my fault at all, and could have been caused by my genes, or even an energy particle from a distant star - I guess we will never know.

Chapter 7
Snake Oil & Insanity Purchases

My husband had been a rock throughout – I was glad we had found each other – and the 'in sickness and in health' vow really came into its own during this time.

He couldn't do enough for me – anything that might ease my stress – he would immediately go and get. He did actually get me a rock at one point – as I had seen a particular internet video channel recommend crystals for their healing properties – call it snake oil or whatever – I was going to cling on to anything that might help, no matter how wacky it was, I'm quite open minded and didn't have much to lose by trying.

There was no question that I was always going to take <u>all</u> the treatment the NHS recommended – but these extra bits helped me to feel like I was doing something – other than sit there like a pudding waiting for doctors' letters.

I got swept along with some channels which said that 'apparently' – rose quartz was going to help my breast cancer – so we went to a crystal shop and bought the biggest boulder of it we could find (albeit it was a second in terms of quality), and every night, I did healing meditations, with my giant piece of rose quartz perched next to my boob.

Doing this gave me a break from wandering around the house saying 'I have cancer' to myself over and over again, and so 'snake oil' was the very first of many insanity purchases.

Something I was warned about – was that I might end up making some ridiculous purchases. I can't remember everything I bought from diagnosis till now, but they have included:-

- Thirty headscarves from car boot sales and charity shops to *balance the flatness of my chest* with my *forever pregnant* looking tummy – I wore them for a short time, but I later learned that my post cancer meds would give me violent hot flushes – so I abandoned wearing them altogether and donated them to a charity shop.

- A selection of hats for chemo – I then didn't need chemo (I did start investigating wigs, but thankfully never bought one).

- Two days post op I bought £45 worth of hideous clothes from a woman at a car boot sale (£45 buys you a lot at a car boot). None of them was suitable – I blame it entirely on the morphine.

- A huge number of pyjamas and jogging bottoms for my kids in a whole range of sizes – 'in case I died or was poorly on chemo'.

- A caravan (sold within months) – I hated it because my husband had to clamber over me to get to the loo – which post boob surgery is terrifying as you're constantly guarding your painful chest wounds.

- A banger of a rusty car to pull said caravan – it survived just two years before being taken to its final resting place.

- A £1000 deposit lost on a static van (decided we couldn't afford to buy it after all and then lost the deposit 'cos the owner looked terrifying).

- My own body weight in herbal tea – that I then became paranoid about in case it was increasing my oestrogen so I donated it to the foodbank.

- A plastic greenhouse and 50 packets of seeds – I decided to 'grow my own', then instantly changed my mind because I was *'a bit tired'*.

- A five-year mortgage tie in – then decided I needed to move house after all, just a week after finalising (£7000 redemption fee).

- A mortifying amount of money on crystals – the more anxious I got – the more crystals I *needed*.

- Four cats and a hamster.

- Hundreds of used books – only a true hoarder could appreciate this collection.

- A tonne of Audiobook credits.

    It would have been cheaper to send me to a retreat in Bali for a year than buying all this stuff.

    The only purchases out of all of that which have been life changing – are my books, and my beloved cats.

    Hence our finances took a hit.

Chapter 8
Eviction Nightmare

Our landlords were older and decided it was time to sell up.

So now we were far flung from anything we knew, were dealing with cancer, and soon to be evicted – brilliant. Just brilliant.

Just when we could have done with battening down the hatches and focusing on family and health, we now had to go hell for leather to find a house to buy.

At least we *could* buy a house, but still, we could have well done without needing to do that 'right now', and money was tight, as we had also hemorrhaged thousands on a high rent on the only house we could find on our one trip to the area prior to moving – the pressure for my husband to start his job was real, so we made an offer on a simple little house and hoped for the best.

Chapter 9
The Booby Show & Tell

What a bizarre experience that was.

I was invited to a 'booby show and tell'. Lots of mostly middle-aged women bustled around a hospital waiting area. They handed out tea, coffee and cake. We swapped stories about everything from *how we found out about our cancer, what treatment we had,* and most importantly – *what we thought of our surgeons.* This seemed to vary spectacularly. I felt incredibly lucky to have a surgeon whom I viewed as a kind 'Teddy Bear', because others were there describing surgeons with the bedside manner of a psychopath.

I got all the juicy details about how one woman's breast exploded – with blood gushing and spurting out down her blouse. Problems with implants, nightmares with breast expanders – I heard it all. I learned all about 'dog ears', which is when you have a mastectomy, and you can be left with fatty squishy lumps dangling under the armpits, because once your fat booby bit from the front is removed – it no longer acts as a weight to the fat you didn't know you had under your armpits – hence post op – your armpit fat springs up like a gert 'Squishy' – I decided I would definitely ask the surgeon not to leave dog ears, that was not going to work for me at all.

The nurse divided us into groups to take it in turns to visit separate rooms which each had a different person who was about to show their boobies to us. Each had a different surgery option, and we could look and ask questions.

The nurse said that in room one, there was a lady who's had 'Diep flap reconstruction', in room two a lady who's had 'LD flap reconstruction' (fat is taken from your flanks because you can't use your tummy due to previous operations), in room three the lady has had straightforward implants.

These women were incredible for doing this – it was <u>brilliant</u>.

We all asked a tonne of questions and inspected the surgeon's work. I noted that *all* the women looked incredible – but I was secretly pleased that *my* particular surgeon's handywork seemed superior which was a huge relief.

At this time, I was sure I would have the Diep flap construction.

Diep flap reconstruction is when they chop off your apron tummy and stick it to where your boob was. First of all, they have to scoop out your boob tissue like ice cream (I thought) and dump it, and then they somehow stick that tummy flap to your front.

The upside to this was that it seemed to come with a free tummy tuck. I had been secretly wishing I could have a tummy tuck after becoming incredibly round after my first pregnancy – and then in time my apron tummy just sagged (partly because I rest the full washing basket on it) and it did not do wonders for my self-image. I tried as hard as I could to focus on how lovely that saggy pouch had been a wonderful home for my beautiful children, how it nourished and nurtured them, but it always came back to the same thing - it looked terrible, and it ruined most of my outfits.

I am unfortunate that my tummy – if I eat too much, not only gets fat, but it sticks out like I'm thirteen months pregnant. Recently, I was asked (with great gusto) if I was pregnant. The woman who asked was clearly well-meaning, and about to launch into great enthusiasm about my 'upcoming birth'. I'm fifty, and whilst that was an inadvertent compliment (I look young enough to bear children) – it was a sore reminder that I really needed to do something about it. But I never did.

Until recently when two devices have made a real impact on my ability to think twice before hitting the snacks. The 'camera' doorbell security system has been a wonderful deterrent to my accessing my fridge. Our fridge is in our garage (don't ask), and should I feel a peck in the night, which is my pattern of snacking (starve all day and eat shite all night), the moment our door to the garage opens it triggers a shrieking alarm, not only waking us and our older neighbours, but four hungry cats as well, hence I only did this once, it was terrifying – and in my half asleep stupor (I take strong mood stabilisers for mental diarrhoea which make me mega drowsy at night) – it resulted in a hell of a shock, an unbelievably poor reaction time, my husband rescued me *star shaped* having fallen *up* my stairs – doped up on my prescription meds I looked like wasted burglar caught in the act.

Another upside to this system, is the fact that the security system videos your ass every time you go out, the app on my phone insists on shaming me in this way – it has been quite a shock for me to dress to go out, check the mirror and think all lumps are covered, only to get a *'woo hoo'* notification from the security company app shouting – *'just to let you know this is what* you *actually look like love'* – and proceeds to show me actual footage of how my backside has an incredibly strange movement when I walk - each ass cheek moves independently of the other – I've never seen anything like it.

I wished I could wear my curves beautifully like so many women do – I'd been diddled out of a sensible height, being petite with genes which would create that 'forever pregnant' physique. I once went for an assessment for a tummy tuck, I absolutely couldn't afford it but went anyway. The bariatric surgeon knelt on the floor, grabbed my doughy paunch and kneaded it into malleable shapes before announcing that I was *'stacked out with fat'*, not just attached to my front, but *'stacked out behind the ribs'* too. What was the point of putting ten grand on a credit card and him lopping it all off then if he wasn't going to get the vacuum in and hoove it all up from inside my ribs.

Having a free 'tummy tuck' however, and a pair of perky boobs was a no brainer.

I totted up how much that would have cost me and felt quite smug at this silver lining that my slug shaped cancer had brought. I decided I would have a breast expander fitted – which is to stretch the skin after the surgeon has scooped out the inside tissue. The expander is an implant that has a device in it that occasionally a nurse can pump up to be bigger with a bit of saline.

I told my doctor that I would indeed have breast reconstruction, and she advised that I would have a 'left side mastectomy' to remove the cancer and all breast tissue, but she would save the skin and stuff an expander in, until my skin had stretched enough to do the Diep flap reconstruction. She wasn't going to be able to save my nipple as my pesky slug was hiding just behind it, but after seeing incredible results at the booby show and tell, including some great tattooed nips – now these were not going to ever be a patch on my nibbly nips, but if we're going to be life or death about it – they'll do just fine.

I undertook some in depth research about the Diep flap reconstruction – however, I was starting to realise that not everyone was happy with the results.

Some loved it – and the results were incredible – you would never know that the person had ever had cancer or a mastectomy – in fact it's perfectly possible to get exactly the size boobs you wanted – the boobs of your dreams with this procedure.

But some results were very different – in some cases – the tummy had been attached to the chest area – but the vessels never joined up, and the area just died and had to be removed, leaving the patient with the flat chest that they really didn't want.

I was told that this surgery was cutting edge – it was microsurgery, and that if I had it done – I would need a nurse by my side for 24 hours (bit intense love - but okay) to temperature check my skin to ensure the transplanted tissue would survive – this was all sounding a bit dodgy to me. Do I really want my own belly strapped to my front, and it 'might die' anyway, and could be life threatening if I got sepsis (which I had post childbirth after bits of my placenta got mangled and stuck in my womb after the midwife had a wrestling match with it).

What a faff, plus I've got two kids, I need to do loads of stuff to do with them - how was this supposed to happen when I'm engaging in tit-fannying operations for months or years of corrections and tidying. I wasn't keen on this dirty big cut across my tummy either – someone said that they wish they hadn't had this surgery because the tummy wound just never really healed that well and they can no longer do sit ups – and even worse – that their tummy had puffed up like a balloon - worse now than what it was pre op. Well, I already looked pregnant – most certainly did not need more puffing up.

By this stage – I was becoming quite iffy about this option. My kids come first, and I definitely <u>did not</u> want to die all for some tummy mangling operation to make a pair of tits.

I couldn't get it out of my mind, that I'm not sure the end result would even 'feel like tits' – as apparently the reconstructions – whichever version you choose just will not leave you with much normal skin sensation – and that can be permanent.

One particular woman said though, that to her utter horror – she discovered post diep flap reconstruction that she had great big hairy flaps. I could barely contain myself – she must surely be of more pure mind than I to keep a straight face, for all I could think of was – well – her great big hairy flaps. She hadn't realised that when they stitched her belly to her front that some of her short and curlies would continue to grow.

The serious point was though – that if you have your belly stuck to your chest – it is likely you will then have a hairy chest. Not just any hairy chest – we are talking a pubey-chest. The pubes at the base of your belly could be stuck to your front – and yes you will have to shave them. This was getting way too Frankenstinian for me – so I went home and didn't think about it for a bit.

Chapter 10

Summary Of Plan From This Point

After the booby show and tell, I decided that the results were all so good that I would park the idea of a flat closure mastectomy after all. I let the team know that I'd opted for Diep Flap reconstruction.

The plan was follows:-

    1. First operation to remove my cancer and insert a breast expander as preparation for operation number two.

    2. Second operation – 'Diep Flap reconstruction' – surgeon to remove breast expander and attach fat from my tummy to shape a breast.

    3. Further procedures such as nipple tattoos and further surgery for cosmetic tidy ups are likely to be necessary, there would be no fixed amount of these as all women heal differently, and some women are keen to have corrections and others just want to run for the hills.

Chapter 11
The First Surgery

The only memories I have of the final lead-up to surgery was feeling panicked when people coughed near my head in shops – they had no idea that they could derail my life saving op with their careless spluttering of dirty bacteria on my head. I got used to showering and changing as soon as I returned from being out just to be on the safe side. If I didn't shower, my OCD would nag me until I did, to be fair – my OCD had a point here – as if someone had just sneezed on my hair, why on earth would I want to then smear said sneeze all over my pillow and inhale it all night.

Then I was reminded that I was going to lose my nipple. Darn.

This really was one of my earliest of worst nightmares. When I was at junior school, I learned in history that 'cutting off nipples' was a form of torture once used in the medieval times – yet here I was about to have the exact same thing.

I waited five weeks for surgery. Wow did I nearly mess that up.

I have a tendency to be difficult to get blood out of, so on the way to surgery to remove the lump, we stopped at a petrol station to grab post-surgery supplies – cake, biscuits, water and orange juice. In my keen-ness to please doctors with my excellent hydration – I guzzled a drink and made my way to the ward. Meanwhile – my husband and children went home to make my bed a comfy nest of pillows, with teddies and presents ready for my arrival the next day.

The nurse that received me to the ward went through a questionnaire – had I eaten or drank anything today? –

'*Yes*' I said.

She looked fearful.

'What have you had?' (her eyes popping out of her head)

'I've just had some orange juice' - I said.

Her face looked ashen, like I'd just told her I'd eaten a full English breakfast – utter horror.

As a former health worker – I felt like a real wally for this – I should know better than to think it's perfectly okay to swill down sugary juice on the way to life saving surgery.

The nurse said my operation may *have to be* postponed – I was devastated.

I cried with all my heart at my stupidity. And there at home was my husband and children – dutifully plumping pillows, carefully placing teddies, chocolates all around my bed, creating a cosy nest for me to recover.

The frosty nurse went off to speak to the anaesthetist – he would discuss my stupidity with the team and make the decision as to whether to save my life today or make me wait (understandably – it was my fault).

The anaesthetist was just twelve years old, or so he looked, and remained composed despite my wailing and soap opera level dramatics.

'My cancer will grow now' I wailed – *'who knows what stage it will be at if you don't take it out today'*.

I cycled round the dramatic story of how I had been trying to aid the staff in getting a cannula in for my op, by hydrating myself en-route, but in my life-or-death stress, I'd inadvertently drank the very thing my medical letter told me <u>not to do</u> and was desperately sorry about it. Which I was - that was all genuine – and I felt wretched.

He went back to the team, they had the discussion, and on his return, he announced that I would indeed go to the ball, *that I was going to have my slug removed today after all.*

He went on to tell me that he would operate in the style of if 'I'd been in a car accident' – that *had I had a car crash*– he would have no way of knowing the contents of my stomach, and so he would do special procedure of a 'bit of pressing on my neck' whilst they intubate me, and it should be okay. Words can't express how grateful I was, I could have given him an action figure there and then, I was so chuffed.

I felt like an absolute turd as the medic drew all over me, I was naked except for granny pants – this did nothing at all to raise my self-esteem after 'orange juice gate'. I have a vivid memory of being startled by their horrific breath, which hit me like a dose of smelling salts. I probably blasted him back with my less than fresh breath too so we were quits there.

They took me to theatre where I predictably gabbled at any staff who would listen – yet again I tried to save as many lives as I could by regurgitating the same cautionary tale.

Staff in theatre were incredibly relaxed and friendly, it felt more like I had just arrived at the pub or something – quite confusing, but oddly the chilled-out vibe worked.

My OCD decided to fixate on the fact that a nurse had taken the *odd decision* to place my outdoor shoes on my clean for surgery bed covers – which I thought was an *odd infection control move* - given they had toilet stuff on the bottoms – since I'd just used a very iffy hospital loo. This was highly upsetting for my pre-surgery brain, but there was nothing I could do – I was going to have to suck up the discomfort and right before one of the most nerve-wracking surgeries I would ever have too – darn those infection control blunders – I could have well done without that worry – can't they just pop them in a bag first or something. No wonder people get bugs in their wounds post-surgery.

Theatre itself was lit up like a cosy drug den – a warm reddish ambience, and they popped me on a wonderful, heated mattress - so when they pushed the drugs through the cannula, I was mightily pleased to go from 'nought to night out' in nine seconds – wow that was good shit. Their joke about the anaesthetist being a 'good barman' was bang on.

The last thing I remember about going into theatre – was just how friendly and chilled the staff were – it was still this 'night out' feel about it – not at all like they were about to chop me up and see my blood, fat and insides.

My OCD then came up with a novel obsessive worry that 'whilst being put out', I '*might*' do something like 'admit to committing a few serious crimes that I hadn't done' – and the more I fixated on it the worse the worry was. Maybe I would admit to a murder or something when I was being brought round – I hoped not, and judging by the staff's faces in recovery they didn't look like this had been the case, and there were definitely no police, which cheered me up no end. These kinds of intrusive thoughts aren't my usual style – but thank you OCD for chucking me this curveball right before a big surgery.

My time in recovery was mostly enjoyable due to the high-quality drugs, though I was swiftly taken to the main ward where I would discover the downside being off my face on anaesthetics.

A note about the nurses – throughout my entire journey – the warmth of nurses varied hugely – some were warm, kind and good listeners, others were cold, *mildly terrifying* and not interested. The warmth and kindness of staff affected how I felt throughout my stay in hospital – I felt incredibly vulnerable and delicate post op.

It's a shame that our NHS doesn't look after its staff as well as it should – they do work hard, and I'm sure many are grumpy just because they are totally burnt out.

One health care assistant couldn't be more stand-offish if she tried, and it made for a miserable vibe on the ward. There's a difference between *being busy* and being just *plain off*. Others were chatty and couldn't do enough, one lovely health care assistant brought me an extra pair of support stockings to take home (one on and one in the wash) and even hung around to meet my kids and say cheerio on my discharge. There are certain members of the hospital team who I'll never forget for their kindness.

Chapter 12
Post Surgery Euphoria!

In a haze, the endorphins had kicked in and I was blissfully happy to have had the slug removed. I was happy and comfy, but stuck in one position, it's difficult to reposition yourself in bed when you're not allowed to push down or put any weight on an arm. I patted around the bed to try to shift position – no luck – then... my right hand felt something strange on the mattress; I examined a small piece of jelly-like stuff on the tip of my finger – 'Could this be a part of my tit?' I thought. I called the nurse – and we both had a look.

'Is this what I think it is?' I said eying it suspiciously.

'Yes, I'm afraid it looks like it' she said.

So, there it was, a memento from surgery, I had finally seen what the inside of my boob looked like. I was quite fascinated by it, so I popped it on a bit of tissue to look at later.

I gazed around the ward trying to establish who I was sharing it with – two younger women, and one older woman was in the bed to my far left – she was quite talkative, had garbled radio on constantly, she called out occasionally, but *off my face on meds* I was unable to respond much, and I was, very exhausted.

I gazed down my hospital gown – my left boob was pale and swollen. I looked at my legs – wtf – they looked like elephant's legs – fat swollen legs, I hoped this would go down. What had they done to them to make them like that? – was it necessary? What if they never go down?

Then I needed a wee, but couldn't get up, so I called the nurse.

Eventually one came, I hobbled to the loo with my drip stand attached, shut the door and undressed – only to discover I'd done a massive horse pee already. Oh dear - no dry knicker sticker for me today then.

Fortunately for me, I was wearing a giant pair of incontinence pants – mini win - yay. I was grateful I'd had the forethought to wear these, since I don't do my pelvic floors at all. I really should because it wasn't long ago that I had a <u>very bad</u> incontinence incident in pound shop.

I don't remember much else about the ward, other than I did finally get to talk to the older woman, she was 92, in the bed to my left. She was a bit further away, tucked away in the corner, but I did – just prior to discharge get chance to talk to her. I had been feeling very sorry for her – she frequently called the nurses, but it took ages for them to arrive, so all of us were taking turns to try to attract a nurse's attention for her. There were times I could see her food perched near to her, but she wasn't eating – my mind wanted to go over and help her, but I couldn't, and I kept nodding off.

Just before I was discharged, I hobbled over to the 92-year-old, who was called Doris. We sat together and had a good old chat. She was beautifully spoken, bright friendly eyes and a very warm heart. I told her about my children; she told me about hers. I had been worried about how much she was eating – because every time the meals came around – she seemed to be asleep. So, I gave her a bag full of cakes, biscuits, and some tissues, wet wipes and my new deodorant spray – she was so thrilled with this – she took hold of my hand and said – 'Do come to see me after you're better dear', and so we swapped contact details, and I was discharged home.

I later discovered – that she was in fact diabetic – my snacks were all sugary carby junk and I could have killed her, what was I thinking!

Despite looking quite a sight on discharge, I was wearing a 'button up the front' purple checked nightshirt, budget supermarket leggings squeezed over my elephant legs, morphined up to the eyeballs I insisted on going around the petrol station mini-mart to pick up ready meals. I didn't want to cause my husband to feel like he had to chef up cordon-bleu meals whilst doing housework and everything else, so a stash of ready meals seemed like a good idea.

I knew he must be tired, he was carrying the can for the whole family, and anything that might help reduce his work seemed to make sense. I felt quite a mess in the shop with my drains swinging in the wind and drips of blood down my shirt, but on morphine I mostly didn't care – apart from when they got caught on door handles jolting a sharp tug on my wound making me want to throw up.

The surgical stockings they give you are quite something – they're clearly made for giraffes given the sheer height of them, if neglected – they will gather up in strange ways creating a whole new style of *side-foot* – their sausage like tightness creating strange clumps of leg sticking out sideways. Not the most attractive and after sporting the fattest elephant legs due to being pumped with what must have been a swimming pool of saline during surgery – my entire shoe collection was never to fit again – I eventually went up a whole size. I don't have many shoes – so this wasn't going to be a huge issue but disappointing none the less.

I arrived home and I could finally sit out in my garden. I'm lucky to have a garden filled with the sounds of birds – one of my many passions. I placed my chocolate bar onto the garden table, took a seat, and was delighted to see a sparrow land on my chocolate bar, not just for a second, but for a few seconds – seeming to do a little dance. I was thrilled to bits with this, and thought that it must be sign, that I am *welcomed home*, it felt like a true gift – I had no idea from where – but I loved it. For years I've wanted a little bird to land on my hand – and here I was with one doing a dance on my chocolate bar – it felt like a sign that things were on the up.

I slowly went through some kind gifts I had been sent, but my initial excitement was dashed when I realised that many of them were likely to <u>increase my chances of a cancer</u>

<u>returning</u> – things that might make me fatter – thus increasing my oestrogen levels. There were essential oils and teas all containing suspicious substances that also might increase oestrogen production (not what I want after having an oestrogen sensitive cancer).

So, the initial happiness at seeing gifts was short-lived, as one by one, I realised that I could not have any of the gifts, unless if I wanted to spend the following week worrying that I might die sooner because of eating them.

The sad thing is, that I had originally asked for the herbal items thinking that *anything natural* must be good for me, but the deeper I delved I realised just how active natural ingredients really are, it was very disappointing as the whole gift box of tea had to be given away, for fear that each sip might affect my health, the worry of it was too much, and for a time I just gave up and drank hot water, as it seemed nothing I put in my mouth was safe anymore.

These days my go-to treat is hot milk, but I do miss my herbal teas, I'm sure many are completely fine, but it's a personal thing and for me and with the lack of robust enough clinical studies I mostly give them a swerve.

For some reason - I struggled with my get-well cards too – they reminded me of sympathy cards, and I didn't want sympathy – my cancer was in the bin, so I was now happy, I felt incredibly lucky to have found my cancer early and get shot of it early too.

A friend popped around with flowers, but they were tricky too – from the initial diagnosis I really struggled with being given flowers – they are of course from wonderful well-meaning people, but they did look *funerally*.[3]

I kept dropping hints that I wanted crystals instead, but the oestrogen increasing substances kept coming. It's upsetting to have to deal with the trauma of cancer, and at the same time be deprived of my comforts, I would have loved to enjoyed tea, chocolate, a glass of red wine – but from this point on those items were all going to cause me more worry than was worth bothering with.

Eventually I told people about these worries – and then I got no gifts at all. I wasn't sure which was better, as I just felt sad.

After this surgery, I wanted to do that *onwards and upwards* thing and announced to everyone that <u>I never wanted to talk about cancer again</u>, only then to continue to mention it constantly for the following three years. As with anything, I reserve the right to change my mind.

Back to the physical bits - I was told to keep the dressings on until the dressings clinic, and until then I had to just shower from the waist down, and I could flannel wash or wet wipe my top parts.

---

[3] Actually, a beautiful friend sent me a rose bush, which feels 100% less funerally, and not at all like half dead flowers. Each year, I watch the roses bloom, which brings me a huge amount of joy to think of it growing with me on my journey towards health. I also just remembered that another friend sent me a sewing kit to make a pretty shopping bag, gorgeous retro print which was unbelievably kind of her.

I was allowed to manage my own drains; I videoed the nurse showing me how to do this as I hadn't trusted my morphine brain to remember anything sensible. Each day I had to empty them and make a note of the amounts of blood lost. They seemed to keep getting blocked which was annoying, a bit of a tap on the bottle sometimes sorted that out.

I decided there was no time like the present to start getting on with life.

Sweating, with my arms feeling barely attached and morphined up to the eyeballs I decided to have a bash at writing a memoir about my cancer journey – not just any memoir though – a memoir with funny bones with a splash of blood. It even had an actual splash of blood on it from my drains.

I had been tinkering around learning how to write over the years, and after creating many a shocking manuscript – I felt that I now had improved enough to give it another go.

I laid back in bed with a laptop propped up and hammered out as much as I could. It was just five and a half weeks post-op that I emerged from my bed stinking yet triumphantly holding a manuscript. Someone was bound to buy this I thought – it was as fresh as my wounds.

I sent the older version of this book out to a few agents and heard crickets. Unbelievable – what does a person have to do to sell a book these days – I had a fully mangled front, I had war wounds and funny anecdotes, I had it all, and still no one wanted it.

It was not until 2024 after taking more writing short courses that I discovered quite how many atrocious mistakes were in that manuscript.

I apologise to any agents who have previously perused my shoddy work – you literally *don't know* what you *don't know* sometimes. Quite right that my manuscript had been passed upon, it was badly written which makes it insulting and timewasting for any reader to be bothered with. Cancer has taught me just how short life is, and I really mustn't contribute to wasting precious moments of other people's lives reading the drivel I've written – they really do have better things to do.

I forget when, but not long after the op I spiked a massive temperature and felt shivery and sick. I went to the Emergency Department wondering if I had sepsis. The Emergency Department was extremely busy, I remember having to listen to some guy in the waiting area drone on and on for hours – it made a miserable situation grim. Do people have to talk *so loudly* and for *so long* when we're in a room full of people feeling horrendous. It's not like you can fully block out the incessant chat out with headphones, as you need at least one ear to listen out for the doc.

I had a cannula fitted to my hand which was the most uncomfortable position – which made the now grim night also painful.

After five hours my bloods were apparently normal, and I was allowed to go home – I must have just had a bug.

The only saving grace to this drawn out night was that I'd brought my earphones in and was able to listen in just one ear – so I was able to enjoy listening to someone else's memoir about cancer which massively helped pass the time – not that's it's necessarily a chirpy or positive book – but it was just helpful to hear about her own journey through breast cancer. The author really seemed to have been through some terrible stuff – so if she can come through it – maybe I can.

It was a relief to listen to books, as I found music difficult to listen to in those early stages – too emotive.

As was finding anything to watch on tv that *wasn't too difficult to get into, wasn't depressing and wasn't quite so full of breasts* as a reminder. Telly programmes full of young women displaying their wares (bikini clad island type gameshows) might not be your go-to telly in this phase – it's going to be a constant reminder of tits tits and more tits.

Back home, I had written in my diary that the first seven days felt like 'darkness'. Audiobooks saved my sanity over and over.

Another diary entry from that time (albeit a bit sparse) was that I'd been *'staring up at the sky, watching clouds form faces and wondering if it was God, and if I'd be meeting him soon, and if I did, would I be floating in the clouds with him. Also, I have a new cough – has it gone to my lungs'*.

To make it worse – I have diary entries that a 'friend' had been giving me the silent treatment around this time. They were being completely weird about answering my call to tell them I had cancer, they were making the stress of my cancer all about *them* and because of that they were not feeling able to take my call. I quickly learned about the term 'cancer ghosting' – great – just what I need.

People's behaviour never fails to shock me, but when they do the silent treatment stonewalling crap on top of your being diagnosed with cancer this takes it to a whole new level of toxic. To make it worse another 'friend' was gaslighting me about the whole thing. I sensed a huge learning curve coming and was absolutely on the money with that.

Chapter 13
Moving House

The recovery process was marred by the fact we were about to move house.

As you would expect – I experienced stress levels through the roof. We found a small and sensible house to buy, we did not have time to look, so it was a temporary house until we knew what we wanted. The move date had coincided with my operation. Just a couple of days after discharge, the removal van arrived - and off my young son and I went to a budget hotel for the day. At least we'll be comfy, I can get food, and rest whilst my husband coordinates the removals I thought.

All went well, my son and I settled into the hotel room and snuggled up to watch telly together. Until he got hungry.

I rang reception to ask if it would be possible to have a meal for my son brought to the room – a flat 'no'.

I persevered – but it was a more determined flat 'no'.

Gutted. I had two drains still swinging, bags of blood, I was now incredibly sore as the anaesthesia had worn off. I had morphine – but barely used it because I was also in charge of a child – so today was not the day to take very strong pain medication – I definitely needed my wits about me.

My son was becoming restless and grumpy as the hangry-ness set in, so we organised ourselves – and slowly, painfully I staggered along the corridors, and we made our way to the hotel restaurant.

By now my young son was really struggling to manage his emotions, and I was publicly struggling to manage to keep him quiet in front of other customers.

I must have looked a stressed, depressed, a pale sickly sight, I probably smelled too, as it was incredibly difficult to wash with the drains attached, I could not use my left arm due to the cut that stretched from my cleavage to my armpit, I had been doing my best – but I felt utterly self-conscious and gross.

In other countries – I think I would not have been discharged yet in all honesty. To top it all, I was now preoccupied with a new and chronic pain in the right side of my abdomen, and so the thoughts that a secondary cancer may have spread to my organs was beginning to cloud my mind and affect my mood. Today the abdominal pain was bad, but I had to put it to one side, put on a smiley face, and most importantly get my beautiful son some lunch.

The waitress came over, she took one look at the sight of the state of me and looked instantly horrified. I struggled again to manage my son's restless irritation, but it was all suddenly overwhelming me – it was too much, the cancer, the house move, what is this pain? Has it metastasised? Was it metastasising due to the stress?

The waitress' voice broke a little – 'was that you – who just rang… about having lunch in your room?'

'Yes – I replied'.

'Oh my God – I'm so sorry' she said.

And with that ounce of sympathy – the floodgates opened, and I was a mess.

A smelly, bloody mess, and it was humiliating.

By now, my son was ravenous – and here I was causing a scene in the restaurant. The waitress apologised over and over, she handed me the menu.

'Tell me what you want – I'll bring it to your room, go on, you both get on and we'll get your dinner to you'.

Still sobbing, my confused son and I hobbled, drains and all back to the hotel room. Not one of my happiest moments.

Our lunch arrived at our room, my son - incredibly fractious by now was delighted to see the food.

Sausages and chips, we ordered sides and puddings too – a good feed-up is what was needed. I just got my son set up to eat his – it looked and smelled great, and he was thrilled, but not for long because the fire alarm went off – I could not believe it.

We were evacuated to the car park, where it was cold, and spat with rain, as we stood out there waiting for ages for the fire brigade.

Our lunch was completely ruined.

I can't remember how we managed after that – it must have been something from the petrol station next door, but it was a horrible day, and it makes me incredibly sad to think about it.

My husband fetched us later in the day, the removals people had gone, and I went home to recover in a house I'd barely set foot in, surrounded by boxes, nothing where we think it is, and a night's sleep made up of all the strange sounds that frighten you when you move house.

The following day – I saw my husband struggling to do everything, it was so frustrating, as I was not allowed to lift anything much, or I could inadvertently dislodge the implant (the breast expander).

I did what I could, but every step was difficult. I emptied the food box into the cupboard – two tins of beans at a time, it took ages – but that was how I was going to be able to help, carrying light things back and forth, whilst sweating, stinking and feeling a bit tender.

I was gutted that I had been cheated out of a luxurious recovery at home, high as a kite on morphine watching history documentaries – instead – this was a period of never quite feeling I could rest for long, because I couldn't bear leaving all the work of unpacking to my husband. We were in a completely new area, it should have been exciting, but it just wasn't, I wanted to be home – but for that matter I'd never known where home was.

Thank goodness we hadn't bought a house we looked at pre-cancer which had absolutely stank of cigarettes. Had I been diagnosed with cancer in *that house* I'd have had a breakdown with the worry of third hand nicotine giving me a secondary cancer – a blessing in disguise as previously I had been devastated at not having our offer accepted on that house.

Chapter 14
The Results

My post surgery euphoria was short-lived due to the hellish wait for the results of the histology from the cancer, as well as the lymph nodes. The results of this meeting could change (or end) my life, quite literally.

In the run up to this appointment my brain decided to torture me by making me think the worst. In *my mind* I could be dead within weeks, as the cancer *might have* spread to every nook and cranny of my body. The surgeon's reassurance of a 'sleepy cancer', quietly morphed in my mind to an aggressive stage 4 cancer. Every ache or pain became a sign that the cancer *might be* eating me up from the inside.

My memories of the appointment to get the results are vague. By this time I was tired and still utterly traumatised by the whole show.

The results showed my cancer measured 2.3cm, instead of the initial 4cm length (estimated at the One Stop Boob appointment).

<u>The cancer was</u>:-

Oestrogen positive

HER2 negative

Stage One

Grade One. (after analysis – it was changed to Grade Two)

Part of my boob got sent to America to be analysed for the likelihood of recurrence.

Apparently, I did not need chemotherapy or radiotherapy – which led me to believe for quite some time that I'd had a *'light dusting'* of cancer. I remember repeating this 'light dusting' to other people for many months after – but now, on reflection, I had not remotely had a 'light dusting' of anything.

Cancer was and still is The mother of all traumas in my life – it has left absolutely no stone unturned – it's ransacked my life to the point it is now unrecognisable – not all for the bad, but still, nothing *light dusting* about it.

When sharing the results my lovely surgeon was very kind and reassuring. They said that they were pleased with the results. I listened to what they said and I felt better, *for a while*.

As the hours, then days, then weeks passed, my mind started whirring again.

What if they missed a bit?

Maybe a few cells got left behind?

Maybe it has spread but they just didn't know it yet?

These kind of thoughts cycle round and round my brain like a washing machine that never stops.

Just days prior to publishing – I had spent some of last night wondering if I had a stage four cancer that just hadn't been found yet, because how can I be *this tired* three years on? It's exhausting – and I wish so much that I could just hand my worries over the powers that be so I didn't have to think about it – but for some reason I just can't – I am at *all times* vigilant due to the unfortunate truth – that that very vigilance found an *incredibly hard to find* cancer once, and that it had indeed saved my life.

If I had allowed anyone to poo-poo my symptoms previously – I may well have been sat in an urn on our fireplace by now.

Chapter 15

The Recovery

As my recovery went on, I became increasingly resentful of my pesky breast expander – that gadget used to prepare my boob for reconstruction.

It made my boob match the other one through clothes – but when naked, my new breast was taut, pale, and odd looking – like it was an implant – but a squared-ish one.

I hated the shape of it, but persevered.

Apparently, I had to get the expander inflated, so pain relief on board (pre-loaded at home) – the nurses pumped me up with saline – my tit grew and grew which reminded me of the enormous turnip – and it was not long after this that the slippery slope of my hate towards that expander commenced.

It was over inflated, and bloody uncomfortable to sleep on, imagine having a flat chest, but you have a large and really firm squishy (kids' toy) shoved under your skin, then lie on your front and try to get comfortable.

I am a front sleeper, I sleep with my hands outstretched – under my pillows, star shaped and, on my front, – and so this 'Frankentit' as I now called it was ruining my sleep.

I then hated the way it was *way too firm*. I became panicky about if it could burst or just leak – what was in it? I tapped my boob skin and couldn't feel *anything* – just numb. I was already numb from nerve damage across great swathes of flesh around my chest, ribs and Franken-tit was starting to aggravate my nerves.

The worse my sleep got, the more I hated it my tit. The numbness drove me round the bend. I had to make sure I didn't stand too close to the hob – as it was so numb it could have caught fire, and I wouldn't have felt a thing.

I had started to look at more horror stories about Diep-flap reconstruction and after looking at many pictures of mangled tummy wounds and necrotising tits – enough was enough – I rang the hospital and said I was done – that I wanted to be flat chested after all.

Chapter 16
Final Decision To Go Boobless

As mentioned earlier – I had been reading a book about a woman who had had a flat closure mastectomy. She looked great in her snappy little blazer jackets – maybe I could have this operation and work towards looking as good as she does, I thought.

My mind was made up – to go flat, was actually what I had *originally wanted* from the earliest diagnosis of cancer – 'take the lot away' was my gut feeling – and I was simply returning to that.

Not as easy as you might think though.

I was originally offered a chance to discuss a right (healthy side) 'Risk Reducing Mastectomy', I thought this sounded incredibly sensible, and so I made an appointment with the breast team to discuss this.

This appointment was very different to the previous ones, which were to discuss which type of reconstruction – in those, my mind remembers them as a montage of photos – of tits, tits and more tits, but my whisper of a mention of just 'going flat' previously was not explored.

I remember telling them very early on that I was happy 'just to go flat', but this thought was closed down. Understandably, as I was in a state of shock at my diagnosis – no time to make radical life-changing decisions involving amputations.

Any good surgeon would encourage a patient to explore all the options and take a long time to think big decisions through. Apparently, it's one of the most common things for breast teams to hear – is newly diagnosed patients telling them to 'take it all away' – so they are right to be cautious.

Here I was, having suffered the severe discomfort of my expander, asking for them to 'remove it, bin it and take the other tit off to match'. I felt considerable push-back on this – I was fortunate that my cancer was apparently a low onco-score (they sent a chunk of my tit to America for a scientist to create a score for how likely it would be to come back). I loved the idea of my tit having its own seat on the trans-Atlantic flight.

The fact of the matter was that there was <u>no good reason to chop off my right boob</u> – it *was* healthy.

But it wasn't as simple as that.

I did not want a life of prosthetics - I did almost the 'full range' of fake accoutrements night clubbing in the 1990's. I used to take ages getting ready to go out clubbing – high heels to fake being taller, make-up to fake looking prettier, Wonderbra – with big puffy pads to make my boobs lift up and stick out, and at times I even wore a huge uncomfortable wig because I wanted to have massive hair (until someone said my head looked too big for my body).

But here in 2022, I was done with embellishing my body to make it look something it is not – if it was going to be at the expense of my comfort, my sleep, not to mention the whole Franken-tit thing was really grating my nerves, and I wanted it OUT.

I wanted to be matching on both sides, and whilst we're at it – I found plenty of examples of women who went flat and discovered post-surgery – that the healthy boob had cancer in it after all, sometimes multiple cancers in it.

That was enough for me – I had decided – the decision was final.

The difference between the reaction you get from your surgical team when you declare 'I want to go flat' feels vastly different to the one you get when you agree to reconstruction.

The push-back as mentioned just now is very palpable (understandably), but to me - the atmosphere changed, and it felt like I'd almost offended them, by not taking the *luxury and popular product* they'd offered me.

A bit like they'd just offered me a top of the range car, all singing, all dancing, but I stood there and said I didn't want it. I was happy with my good old reliable grandad car, it starts every time, it's easy to drive, and never lets me down. To which they say 'okay' then slam the door in my face. They of course did not really do this, but it felt like it to me.

I was sensitive and needed support – just because I didn't opt for the 'fancy tits' option – didn't mean I didn't need support – but there was little to nothing.

It felt like once I embarked on this path, the door was slammed, and I was on my own.

No nurse to comfort me about my decision - *you make your bed – you lie in it* is how it *felt* - but if you change your mind and want fancy tits - come back and we'll shower you with photos, exciting plans and lots of support.

So, Instead I joined a 'flattie' group online – but they only allow pre-flatties to be a part of the group for one month (to explore the idea) and then they politely close you to access to that group.

I did discover that they do offer fantastic support once you are *through the other side* – the flat-side. I just didn't understand this policy at the time, I probably hadn't read the small print, and I felt excluded – no real support anywhere except my husband, my handful of kind friends at the other end of the country.

Looking back now, I think I understand why the group says cheerio pre surgery – because like anything, some of us can be persuaded by lots of positive stories that a particular surgical option will suit us, we get caught up in other people's success stories and get swept along with the tide.

A flat closure mastectomy is no small matter – it's life changing mega surgery and definitely not for the faint hearted.

I now thank that little flattie group for temporarily and politely closing the door to me, as it gave me time to really think the option through for me, without influence.

And sure enough, when I was through surgery, they welcomed me straight back in no questions asked, but at least I knew that the decision had been mine, the buck stopped with me and I could never blame anyone else for persuading me that mega surgery was a good idea when they don't know me. That group went on to be a mine of brilliant information and warm support, for which I am very grateful.

I started looking at as many other 'flat and happy' groups online as I could - these groups were more about 'what to wear once you're a flattie' – more about this later on, but in a nutshell – what you will be able to wear will likely change, there are lots of options and it's quite fun to rethink your wardrobe. It's all about drawing the eyes up to neckline ruching, or jewellery or halter necklines and avoiding the obvious low-cut clothes – unless if you can still get away with that – in which case – brilliant!

For me, the honest reason to go completely flat, was about reducing risk of recurrence. I had always wanted children from a very young age, I miscarried in my teens, but despite it being an unplanned pregnancy, I had wanted that baby more than anything in the world, and experienced utter trauma and devastation at the loss of her, I'm still upset about it now.

I wanted to be a young mum, who grew alongside her kids, and had plenty of time to be with them. But I wasn't'.

I was now much older, and it felt too painful that time could run out already – it felt like – what? – but *I've only just got going*, I've got my kids, but they're just young – what about seeing them get married, have kids, it just felt unbearably unfair.

Back to my journey towards getting a double mastectomy agreed - I learned quickly <u>not to mention</u> the 'risk reducing' aspect of my wanting to go flat – that would be shut down by the breast team in an instant.

Quite bizarre – as the surgery is called 'risk reducing mastectomy' but the minute you mention that – (depending who you speak to) – they can get quite irritable, unless if you have a combination of reasons for needing that a healthy breast to be removed.

My own doctor (the teddy bear) was wonderfully kind, but I did feel somewhat terrified of the second opinion doctor he seemed to look furious that I should want to mutilate myself in this way – resulting in longstanding body issues and chronic pain possibly forever.

I did, however, learn that if I said I wanted the surgery for 'symmetry' then my wish *might* be granted. This was actually also true for me – as there was no way I wanted to wear a prosthetic boob/knitted knockers or anything like it. I did order some, tried them once and never again did they see the light of day – they just rise up and start to peek out your top at people – I don't care how many ways there are to make them stay put – they are just not for me.

I was warned online of the post-surgery pain, that the pain could go on for a long time, that I could experience a feeling of tightness across my chest – I'd heard some people call it 'banding' like a belt pulled way too tight. I was warned that it may not be the lack of boobs that would get to me – but how much my tummy (my 13-month pregnant looking one) would *appear* stick out more.

I was also warned of something called 'phantom nipple syndrome' – I was pretty sure I *wouldn't* get that – surely *sensible people wouldn't get that*.

It was a cold, miserable and painfully lonely quiet road towards my double mastectomy.

I had to wait till the following June but was pleased the date was now on the calendar, and soon I'd be free of that darn expander – and I could sleep happily once again, ahh, I missed my sleep so much.

At this point – people were confused as to why I was having a mastectomy, when I had just had a mastectomy – and I could either go into great detail about the tale of the expander being a nightmare – or just look a bit of a wally – they really looked quite confused and it became a little tiring working out what to say.

Chapter 17

Doris

Doris, the now 93-year-old from the bed next to me on my first op (the diabetic one I gave a bag full of cakes too) appeared to have survived the vast array of inappropriate snacks I had left her and got in touch, and from there – a most unexpected but beautiful friendship began.

Doris started to phone me weekly, and a warm supportive friendship started to grow from there. We had no past, who knows how much future, but it didn't matter, if anything the lack of history probably helped.

I had felt increasingly disconnected from people around me – it is almost impossible to call anyone anymore – we seem to be busier now than in the 1980's when I used to be able to 'just call someone'. Are we all busier? I wasn't sure. But hardly anyone actually wants to talk anymore, and I felt it.

It made me deeply sad in my heart that here I was dealing with a 'life changing diagnosis' – and in the end it at times felt no one cared. Of course people *did* care, and my inner circle were stellar supporters, but sometimes that didn't feel quite enough, and I'd like for those who I texted my devastating news, or read it on my then social media to have dropped me a line to check in – but rarely did they do this – preferring to respond *in line* to my initial post where I said that I had cancer. It felt like initially this was just 'interesting on a popcorn-eating gossipy level' – but beyond that, people had 'scrolled on' to the next post or ten and forgotten it. Heaven forbid I ever attempt to see them in person – what a performance that would be.

Again, in hindsight – I would have to wonder what I brought to that table – how many times had I checked in on other people – to see how their surgery had gone or find out if they were feeling brighter after a period of depression – but I hadn't. So, it was one-all, in the age of social media we hadn't cared for each other, and that was that. It felt like everyone was staring at social media and it was like talking to people with bloody great cloth ears, and I had been one of them.

Doris, however, was time rich, and I was connection poor.

Here I found connection with a now 93-year-old woman in a nursing home. I was soon to discover though, that Doris was so much more than just this.

Our chats became more frequent. All our conversations were by telephone, actual phone calls! Except one where I visited her at her nursing home. On the phone, you would never know that Doris was 93. She had a beautiful voice, was so kind, and was the best listener you could ask for. It was like going back to the 1980's.

Initially it was strange talking to someone I didn't know *that well* took a lot of focus to relearn some lost skills over the years of being able to hold a sensible telephone conversation with someone I barely knew.

The more I spoke to Doris, in my mind – the younger she got.

By some months along it felt like I was simply talking to someone the same age as me. Doris was able to be 'present' whereas so many people cannot be. Doris didn't keep checking notifications, she didn't keep making me wait whilst she read messages, and didn't catch sight of any posts that were so cutting edge she had to interrupt me to glance at it before she could possibly hear me out, neither did she reply to text messages in between pretending to listen to me like so many people casually do these days.

Looking back – it feels like there is an argument for matchmaking for people in nursing homes with people of all ages, if you could get past all the obvious screening issues to root out people wanting to take advantage that is.

How lovely would that be – to match up people of any age who are struggling to feel connected – to the wonderful humans we have sat around in residential and nursing homes - with all that wonderful wisdom, life experience and a big dollop of interesting and funny stories to tell.

I loved hearing about Doris's earlier years – she was like a living history book – I was hearing real history from the horse's mouth; she had some fab anecdotes too – it felt like a real privilege.

I feel such sadness when I think of all the souls gone by, it makes my tummy turnover to think how painfully sad it is that millions of beautiful souls are no longer here to share their stories. It feels like a tragic loss – and only for them to end up in nursing homes on a production line to get dressed/have breakfast and sit in a day room at a nursing home – it just doesn't feel right.

I hadn't felt this so acutely before cancer. Something about the sadness of having that glimpse of how you actually feel when you might be about to depart earth – it gave me a profound empathy for those about to leave this world and made me quite sad.

Chapter 18
Managing Information

About this time, I started to change the way I manage my own information and seriously question why I was sugar coating news and trying to manage other people's mental health – surely that was *their* responsibility.

Initially – I was so careful to *baby the news* to certain people, not wishing to cause any undue worry, but this after a while, became such a massive albatross that I decided to bin that approach and not ever sugar coat any news ever again.

I was having enough trouble processing updates myself let alone trying to take responsibility for other people's mental health.

I also discovered that…

<u>There is a difference between those who support you and those who *think they are supporting you.*</u>

For some people – hitting 'buy now', walking off and letting delivery companies push gifts through your letter box feels like help. But as mentioned previously – it was good listeners that I was after, but this was trickier than expected to obtain. I didn't really want presents, I wanted connection – real connection with someone who hears me, empathises and gets me. I was so appreciative that a friend who lived miles away took so much trouble to visit me in person twice – what a luxury that was to sit in the garden with a genuine friend – the hug she gave me was priceless.

People made all sorts of excuses *not to* pick up the phone.

As mentioned earlier - 'cancer ghosting' was real.

And apparently my cancer was 'stressing' a particular more distant friend out – unbelievable. Whilst I would accept this from my own immediate family, I don't accept that my cancer could much stress people out who barely have a modicum of an idea of what my life is like – it seems that the most peripheral of people will latch onto the drama of your cancer in order to gain sympathy for themselves, hard to believe, but very much true.

I learned that your cancer journey can become *supply* to some people.

Some people are only interested in the Shaeden Freuden catastrophes in your life will devour bad news because it energises them.

You'll spot who these are because once you start dusting yourself off and doing better, they won't be the slightest bit interested.

If people are sat around *discussing you* – but not actively picking up the phone and offering any remotely human support, and I'm not talking gifts – then there is a chance your news has become supply – an endless amount of interesting negative information that in some weird way makes them feel relieved they are doing better than you.

There will also, unfortunately, be people who blame you for your cancer, again, this crap is the gift that keeps giving.

Apologies for going negative Nancy on you, but I can't sugar-coat this crap – it hurts deeply when people are unkind at the very time when you need the most comfort.

Chapter 19

Keeping Going

My chats with Doris highlighted what was lacking in my life, where my time was going down the toilet.

I became disheartened by the shallowness of social media, so I mostly uninstalled those accounts.

It's the combination of lack of privacy, the icky-ness and the sheer volume of unbridled rudeness which tipped me over the edge – I mean honestly, what was the point.

I started to think about what else I could do with my time, in between helping the children do stuff, cleaning the loo, feeling chained to the sink, way too much washing for it to be normal, and taking care of our four cats – I was on a personal development mission, and it started all with audiobooks.

I had tried so many times over the years to read actual paper books – but was having a nightmare with being able to concentrate. I seemed, like so many others I hear about, just not to be able to focus on even one page enough, to be able to get to the next page. It was very annoying and was making me feel quite thick.

Until I discovered audiobooks from the library. These changed my life. I no longer had to read the same line over and over until it made no sense anyway – I could press play, and a wonderful actor would read it with intonation in all the right places – brilliant! – so I got obsessed with it. I even obsessively listened to books encouraging me to be obsessive – it was brilliant – I'm good at that.

There seemed to be an inordinate amount of housework to do every day - so I lined up a few books, popped my earphones in and off I went. Mission achieved – as I was soon flying through books and really learning some useful stuff.

Books became my new obsession, and the brilliant thing was, that now I had binned off much of my social media, the only thing I could do was listen to audiobooks, with the exception of one social media which I eventually paid for ad free due to the vast educational content.

After listening to hours of audiobooks, a strange thing happened, which was somewhere along that line, I got my concentration for reading back!

As in reading *actual* physical books. I had built up my concentration and it had become strong – hurrah!

With renewed enthusiasm, I started to scour charity shops and dusty book shops for gorgeous vintage literature, a pastime I'm still enjoying at time of writing.

Worth noting that I once had an 'issue' with being on a bit of the wrong end of the spectrum of hoarding.

What a horrible word. I prefer to think of it as I'd just *bought too many things for the size of my house* – that sounds *much* better.

It's very hard, because I have so many interests, and my favourite pastime is to furnish those interests with the items I need to do them – like craft, reading, sewing. The only problem is, when I get stressed, I start to lose track of how much time I will actually have to *do* any of these hobbies.

I've calculated previously that I'd need at least two lifetimes to get through my 'to be read' books, another lifetime to learn how to do 'pattern cutting' and 'dressmaking' to the level I would like, and another lifetime to become much more proficient cheffing in the kitchen, and then another one after that to learn how to make electronic dance music, and just one more after that to create some miniature dolls houses. There really isn't enough time to get it all done.

Whenever considering a new hobby – I do have to have a word with myself about how much time I realistically have to do it, and what will it be at the expense of.

My husband built some bookshelves and my collection grew. Thankfully not too large at time of writing but at a pound a book and sometimes cheaper – give it time.

Chapter 20

The Crap Advice

Obviously, what's crap advice to me, might be brilliant advice to someone else – but here's some of the suggestions of things that will help my cancer journey that went straight out the window.

Cold Ice baths - uh, nope, definitely not, although at least I wouldn't have the nibbly nip issues now.

'No sugar' – I don't think so.

Abandon NHS treatments and go purely homeopathic – nope.

And then there was the *mother of all* advice that avalanches upon newly cancer patients – it's a biggie, it's - 'Death by Keto'.

If you are freshly diagnosed, then something to prepare for, is that people - often people you barely know – will try enthusiastically to get you to adopt a keto diet.

It becomes one of many things that become increasingly taxing to hear when you are struggling enough as it is.

Unsolicited advice is well documented to be top of the list of annoying crap that random people do 'to you' (I'm guilty as charged) – but this one particularly irked me – as people never stopped to ask if this was the particular sales spiel I wanted to hear.

What people *didn't know* – is that I was *already* on keto when I got cancer, and I had been on it for a year.

Whilst I'm not saying for moment that this was related – they were preaching to someone who was feeling unsafe about just about every food, substance, chemical that went near me let alone the fact I now felt worried that I'd been eating weird food in the lead up to cancer.

There's something about telling a person you have breast cancer that seems to draw out the most bizarre and inappropriate comments from people. I can't even say it was manageable at first – it wasn't.

I was at my most sensitive on diagnosis, and yet all manner of suggestions that I 'needed to *'take a look'* at what I had been *'doing wrong'* to get my cancer in the first place – how blooming rude and thoughtless.

We already know about the things that might have caused our cancers, can we be at least spared the shaming about it, to this day I'm never far away from someone who is more than happy to dehumanise me about my own cancer – how wonderful.

I was then encouraged to engage in groups that promoted 'natural healing' (does that mean I shouldn't have the NHS treatments then?) and a myriad of other snake oil alternatives that I was not remotely interested in.

I get that people want to help but often help isn't suggesting the thing that 'they' would go for if it was them – because I am not *them* – I am entirely different.

I am not averse to a bit of snake oil; I loved meditating with my boulder of rose quartz next to my boob – I really believed it was shrinking it. I didn't care if anyone thought this was nonsense, because it was *my nonsense* and it helped me to get through my own trauma. It's something to do with feeling like you might be possibly doing something to help yourself, and that mind control - focusing on the cancer shrinking, truly helped me at that time. Do I believe in crystals now? Probably not – but they are still beautiful, and I thank them for helping me through an incredibly traumatic time. Choose your own snake oil and I'll choose mine thank you very much.

The next phase of comments included - 'It hasn't spread then?' – ugh – well thanks for putting the idea it might spread; I'd forgotten about it until you said that.

People are obsessed with this and have no regard for your feelings when they demand to know. We don't want to think about it, and if it *has spread* then I'll let you know *if I want to*, and while we're at it please don't ask me about this in the middle of the supermarket.

'So, the cancer is gone then?' - Is the next gem.

Well, '*I don't have it currently*' I reply – 'so it is gone then?' they ask again, as if I heard wrong the first time.

They are looking for the certainty of a scientist, but I cannot give it. I would love to know too, believe me, but I don't.

So, they look at me like I'm desperately trying to cling onto my cancer identity – but I'm like - no, I just don't want to tempt fate.

Please don't tell me 'it's gone then!' - like I should feel safe sound and can run for the hills – life after cancer is a long and incredibly lonely path of hyper-vigilance and for some, can be a misery of health anxiety – you don't just chop it out then smile like an inane chimp – like many things in life it just isn't that simple.

Re the looming flat chest – someone online in the earlier days said - 'It's lucky you found a partner before you got it then' – thanks – yes, my poor husband will never find me attractive again then – thanks for giving me a new anxiety to obsess about – I'll chuck it in the bag with the rest.

'How will you manage in the bedroom?'

'Well, how do you manage in the bedroom?!' I feel like asking.

Do you mean *'how will my husband manage with nothing to grab onto?'* – well how does yours find you attractive when your personality is annoying – if we're talking about being passion killers we can swap notes.

Why on earth didn't you get the tummy tuck?

Because it turns out it isn't a tummy tuck.

Why didn't you take the boob job?

Because it turns out it isn't a boob job either.

I want to ask, 'why are you nosy' and then state that this is cancer we are talking about, not cosmetic surgery, and these operations will be a brutal assault on my body in an attempt to *not die*.

What's the point of having perky tits and cool abs if I'm on the slab. (I don't mean this to be unkind to women who are going for reconstruction, it's just that the interrogation becomes unmanageable at times, and as my patience becomes paper thin, my internal answers become more blunt. Of course, for most women – having reconstruction will offer just as much protection as going flat would have, but I'm just sharing my inner thoughts which can be how I feel at *those times*).

I wouldn't want anyone to feel that I mean they are shallow for wanting that flat tummy or perky pair of boobs, I wanted it too. But these questions can become infuriating for a flattie which tests my patience at the best of times.

Ultimately, it's all just invasive, violating and I don't want it any of it. It reminds me of when I was pregnant and quickly changing body was discussed and patted by all manner of strangers like it wasn't my own. I honestly don't know which is worse, I just don't want any of it, I want *my* boobs.

Chapter 21
A Dabble With Religion

I experimented with looking at different religions since cancer, which is a very new thing for me. I discovered a whole world of support via our local church which is incredibly kind. They welcomed us in, and I always felt like they caught us, like a safety net to help us cope at one of the most devastating times of our lives. I remain open minded about Christianity – sometimes I read parts of the Bible, sometimes I read about Buddhism – I enjoy taking any parts that help and letting go anything that doesn't. I have also discovered an interest in philosophy, which is also helpful for me to try to gain new perspectives about life.

A first for me – a most surprising one at that – I rocked up at my local church. The appeal of crystals was waning, and I was wandering and wondering spiritually if there was anything else out there that was going to fill this 'thing'... a space, a void, just something not right, or something missing. Couldn't put my finger on it but I went anyway.

Coming from an outsider's perspective, as in I have no idea anything about Christianity whatsoever, attending church was an interesting experience stuck with it and went weekly for ages. We were in a strange area, knew hardly anyone – and quickly church became the thing that punctuated our week.

People regularly asked how we all were, smiles, hugs, were gratefully received, and it went from not just punctuating our week, but being the highlight of it. We went to picnics, were invited for walks, and we made some fantastic friends that we will know for life. All in all, it was a huge surprise to challenge myself, learn so much, and those gains keep coming. but I won't go on about it in this book, I'm sure you get the idea – person joins a church and goes on to have a few interesting spiritual awakenings type thing.

I did however have a painfully difficult time, around Christmas, just seven months post op. I had a cluster of worrying symptoms which needed to be investigated, but it all came at once, right on top of Christmas. I went through untold physical pain in the week prior to Christmas and had to wait until January for my results.

It was agonising. I struggled mentally so much at this time, we went to church, but it was just too difficult. The emotive music at church hit me so hard, and I already felt like an outsider looking in. I was convinced I had secondary cancer, and seeing my husband and children at church I had the most surreal experience of feeling as if I was outside a window, peering in to see the three of them, without me, just as they would be if I died.

I cried uncontrollably during that service and had to leave immediately. From that time on, the music was always difficult for me because it hit a part of me that just talking couldn't access. I got fed up with crying at church and causing a scene, and amongst a couple of practical reasons, I parked going for a bit and we returned to car boot sales on Sundays like we'd never been away.

For a while, finding comfort in Christianity was like a rock, it was a stable base to come back to. Something reassuring about doing the same thing every week and lovely to get hugs too.

I'm sure some people I know must have thought I'd lost it when I started banging on about going to church, some people are so mean, unwilling to try new things for themselves, preferring to sit on their sofa complaining about other people's choices.

I remain open minded about religion to this day – I won't bang on about it but you get the idea.

Chapter 22
Clinical Psychology

The double mastectomy with flat closure had been agreed in principle, and the surgical team did their due diligence and organised two psychological assessments.

Both took place on the phone. I spoke to a wonderful clinical psychologist – who interrogated the corners of my mental state in the nicest possible way she could.

Lots of stuff around how would I cope with my new body image?

Is my partner supportive?

How will I cope with long term pain that may last forever?

Both telephone conversations were long, but incredibly supportive, and if I needed support post-surgery, at any time, she encouraged me to let the cancer team know straight away.

I was feeling all set for surgery.

My hatred towards the expander increased, and finally a few days before surgery it was really hurting, an ouchy stinging pinching feeling – very unpleasant and I was ecstatic to soon have it out.

It felt like an unbelievably long wait for surgery – I think they do this on purpose to make sure it isn't a knee jerk reaction.

Once that date loomed within ten days – I felt a deep escalating panic about having my healthy boob removed.

And so, the final ten days was an increasingly dark, tense and hideous time – I had entered the abyss, and it was impossible to know if I was doing the right thing.

Chapter 23

Enter – The Abyss

I've never felt dread like I felt this. It was so bad it deserves a chapter of its own.

The anticipation of chopping my boobs off was horrifying.

Truly 'dark night of the soul' stuff.

I was chopping my breasts off to live longer for the children – I did not want any of this, but if it gave me the very best chance of not ever getting this diagnosis again it would be worth it.

The double mastectomy date was very close. Having the painful expander removed was a good thing – but having my healthy breast removed was starting to feel completely insane.

A heavy feeling gnawed at me daily, and worsened the closer the op came. I was consumed by fear.

One thing that I did do to try to balance the trauma of losing my frontage, was to get my hair dyed blonde. The aim was to counteract the loss of looks with something that pepped me up a bit. The unfortunate thing was when booking the appointment, I cried my eyes out – again.

Splattering my drama all over the hairdresser's reception area – I had only meant to nip in to make that appointment, but once I uttered the words 'I'm having a mastectomy, I might feel less bad if my hair is nice' I caught sight of the hairdresser's pity and out poured the tears again.

By this time - it was impossible to talk to people about it in any way that was helpful. No one could relate to it, it sounded bizarre – to cut off a healthy boob… Why would anyone do that?

And then there was Doris – Doris continued to phone me; she had had a flat closure mastectomy on one side and was able to offer the most wonderful support.

I wouldn't listen to reassurances from anyone else, just Doris.

By the final week pre-op, my husband had some time off, and all I could manage to do was take myself up to my comfy cosy bed, where I'd shut the door and made a lovely nest, with cups of tea, a stack of books I'd been putting off reading, and I rested. The worry about removing both breasts was all consuming, and just getting through those days was exhausting.

Thank goodness my husband was able to give me that space – he took care of the kids – while I took care of me. Doris – at age 93 - was just the rock I needed.

I progressively felt the worst I'd felt in years, panicky, frightened and there she was – a complete stranger had rocked up and provided a connection I could not get anywhere else.

Those last couple of days prior to surgery were harrowing – yet Doris still called. 'Come and see me when you're better dear' she said.

We planned the most wonderful get-together - she said, 'yes dear – we shall have a jolly good natter!' I knew little about Doris, she had lived in Cornwall, she adored her family, and she too loved cats. It wouldn't be long before we could fill in the rest of these gaps – getting to know this stranger was like a painting by numbers, where only a few sections have colour – the rest to be discovered. I very much looked forward to seeing the full picture soon – lovely to have something to look forward to after the op.

My nerves had really kicked in that last day prior to the op.

The final two days were just one dark extended panic attack. Definitely not a good time to be making big decisions.

I was glad to be able to isolate and do my thing pre-op. I needed that headspace to make sense of it. I didn't feel chatty, I didn't need to hear other people's thoughts or opinions, I just needed solitude, all bar daily calls with Doris.

I projected every attribute I could ever want in a friend onto Doris, and she lived up to it perfectly. She was a warm and thoughtful listener, she never seemed to judge, and best of all was generous with her time – what a luxury that was, in a time when no one speaks on the phone anymore, and if you email someone – they direct you to their social media feed for you to catch up – how nice.

Chapter 24

Second Surgery – The Double Mastectomy

This time was different.

A solemn feel to the hospital, a feeling that permeated onto the surgical ward.

Stark white, bright lights replaced the warm red ambience in the operating theatre this time.

The surgical trolley was sparkling with an array of sterile, sharp and shiny surgical instruments. Did they really need to parade these ferocious looking instruments when I hadn't had a drop of anaesthetic? The strip lighting was sickly bright; I couldn't stop looking at that trolley and I was starting to get panicky – very panicky.

The staff were busy, not as warm.

There was an air of importance around this surgery – well it was a longer and more complicated one I guess, and this reflected in the seriousness of the staff. If the last surgery felt like a night out at the bar, this one felt like I'd woken up in a horror film.

Why couldn't it have been the other way round? This surgery was far more brutal than the last one.

My eyes kept flicking over to the exit door, was it too late? Something felt off, really sinister, but I didn't move, to me – I had no choice.

I was previously excited about having some more morphine and looked forward to being off my tits (pardon the pun) on anesthetic. Imagine my disappointment on discovering that this time I woke in searing agony.

I woke as I was still being wheeled out of the theatre and a fiery rage of pain ripped across my chest area making me feel violently sick. I don't think that was meant to happen, but apparently the fine line the anesthetist treads to balance patients feeling 'off their face' and 'in agony' is a tricky one – I'd lost out this time and got the wrong end of the bargain.

Thankfully the recovery nurse was absolutely on her game and as a team we worked through the agony and brought that pain down to manageable – what an absolute legend she was – she knew exactly what to do and she did it fast.

'What number pain are you?' – 'ten' I said... she pushed in some pain relief...

'what number now?'... 'nine' I said, and 'I'm gonna be sick', cue the sick bowl, and on it went until the horror subsided.

Oh wow, I hadn't expected that, I felt lucky to be alive at all after that.

On the ward I was a hot sickly mess. I felt like one of those patients you see on telly all bandaged up and can't move – it's just a very strange and helpless feeling to not be able to change your position in bed without having to plan each maneuver with military precision. Of course, the nurses are there, but they are also incredibly busy, I certainly did not want to press my call bell every time I needed to move a bit.

Eating my tea was tricky, roast dinner with sprouts. And as I realised that unfortunately one of my large breast dressings was flapping in the wind – it had not been sealed across the top at all – all I could think was how I definitely *did not* want that hot steaming sprout landing inside my dressing, which was trickier than you think because when you lean forward to put the food in your mouth, the dressing gaped open – yuk.

And to make it worse, I really did not want to see what was going on under that dressing, a gooey hot red oozing wound.

After a horribly uncomfortable sleep, the next day they said I could go home, so my husband again came to collect me.

It was a long old walk to the car park, and unfortunately my husband kept banging my wheelchair into kerbs, and the car managed to find as many bumps as it could find on the way home. Without boobs – there's nothing to jiggle – yet that pain was still oddly unpleasant.

At home, my wonderful husband and children had again made a lovely cosy nest of pillows for me. Such a huge help when it's hard to use your arms, at least if you can't weight bear, you can at still lean on one side or another to relieve pressure.

Days later, I was again told to remove my dressings way quicker than I thought was appropriate – and to shower over the wounds too – what? Oh wow – the shock of my disfigured body floored me.

My whole body was still swollen from the intravenous meds, my tummy distended (why does that happen post-surgery?)

I looked t e r r i b l e.

There was little to crow about that the expander had finally gone – my unsightly wounds and puffy body looked shocking.

To make it worse, my clothes kept sticking to my wounds, so I started wearing a simple cotton vest. I think this was to help me pretend I didn't look the way I did - just as much as stopping the wounds getting stuck to my night shirt.

My wound was still oozing like a cheese toasty – the thought of it sticking to all my clothes made me feel gross.

You are supposed to wear a 'button up the front' nightie because you can't lift your arms above shoulder level without risking dislodging some of the sutures inside, let alone the outside. Not far along, it is perfectly possible to just wear oversized stretchy nighties, I preferred these in the end as I like a bit of stretch in my nightwear rather than cotton which doesn't have much give in it, especially when it's not easy to reposition when your nightie gets twisted in bed.

A difficult few weeks passed – which mostly involved a cycle of codeine, morphine, thinking I look terrible, but generally being incredibly grateful to be alive.

Chapter 25

Post Surgery Recovery

In terms of ongoing support from the team, I felt kicked off the conveyor belt faster than a budget supermarket checkout.

No follow up, no nothing, well after the wound check barely anything.

Another punishment for going against them and having the surgery they didn't want me to have I thought. I was alone at home trying to come to terms with the state of my frontage, and it was *horrible*.

I was devastated at the lack of aftercare, but remembered how stretched the NHS was. The staff *have to* prioritise those who need operations to remove 'actual cancers'. I guessed they just didn't have the time to fanny about smoothing past patients, who at least were *somewhat out the other end* and at least had a chance at going about their 'normal' business any time soon.

It was a chance call to the breast care team some months later, when I struck upon a breast care nurse who was working from home. She had something that the rest of the team did not have – time! I had a wonderful chat with her, she listened, and heard, and smoothed, and I felt so much better – so they *did* care after all! I thought.

She said – 'we don't tend to hassle patients once they've had all their surgeries, we let you get back to your lives, but just know that we are always here okay, any time you want a chat, have a worry or just want to ask us something – just call'.

If only I'd heard that in the months previous.

Better late than never, and even this week, almost three years post cancer I can say that I called the breast care team and had a wonderful call with a member of staff, who offered a lovely bit of reassurance about a niggle about op three I had.

Underscoring all of this, is that my surgeon removed my (slow growing) cancer within just five weeks of having that cancerous biopsy result. That was the main thing, and I can never thank her enough for that - she saved my life, and for that, I will be forever grateful.

Chapter 26
Further Surgery Issues

Oh wow - a double mastectomy really hurts. And it hurts for AGES.

You get a whole cocktail of numbness, shooting pains, electric shocks, nagging aches. My 'healthy' side was so much more painful than the cancer side – I guess because there was already existing nerve damage on my cancer side which reduced the pain I felt on that side for the entire recovery.

The gap between my scars, where the cleavage used to be, was missing post op, there seemed to be no gap at all, maybe the tiniest of gaps – I was gutted.

I don't mind having two horizontal lines across my chest, but I definitely don't want just one continuous line *arm to arm* as for some reason, I didn't think this looked great for me.

Over time, as the wounds tightened (a lot!) and healed up nicely – there was a lovely gap again (where my cleavage used to be) – phew!

It was immediate post-op though when I started to feel the longer term physical and psychological issues start to wear away at my self-esteem – in fact the worst of this trauma hits you immediately when you see yourself in the mirror, it was quite a nasty shock, and would take some months to get my head around.

I had <u>really</u> bad cording.

Cording is something weird – where these *what look like* 'wires' pop up from your wound site and radiate all over your torso in all directions. They just kept popping out at me, each day I looked in the mirror there were more. The worst thing was that they were *very* painful, they pull tight like the tautest of strings and restrict your already restricted movement.

So, if your mangled armpits don't stop you stretching – your cording definitely will.

Sharp electric shock type pains drove me crazy. They kept me awake at night and ruined any chance of a comfy recovery on my lovely bottle of morphine.

Just my sodding luck to, that my right drain sat bang on one of my cords – it was agony, just agony.

I spoke to the district nurses about it, but they really didn't seem to understand what I was saying – I would have had more sympathy from the postman.

Eventually, after much pain relief they finally did remove the drains. The left one was not sat on cording and slipped out with virtually no pain, and no problem, but the right one – I was almost through the roof with agony. I usually have a high pain threshold, but this was way too much.

I was immensely pleased to see that right drain it go; it had been the bane of my recovery.

And the stress of trying to get the district nurses to comprehend why one drain was more painful than the other was almost as bad as the pain itself – a sort of mental pain at not feeling listened to or understood. Why do they not know or seem to care about cording, or at least how painful it is if it's pressing on a nerve.

I was gutted – You tell people you are hurting, and it feels like they shrug their shoulders. I thought they were supposed to validate my pain, offer some information about it, or show they care, but the lack of response from the district nurses was heartbreaking – I was in agony, and it looked like they could not have cared less. Burnout is the most likely cause I guess – it's not exactly a mystery that our health services are buckling under the strain of lack of investment. I bet most of the grumpy staff went into their jobs with a great attitude, and wanting to help as many patients as possible – but instead buckled under the strain of it all.

I'm aware that health staff have so much admin to do it's a nightmare – a patient only has to fart and it has to be documented in five places. And a nurse enjoying a leisure-poo is likely to trigger a referral to HR. I exaggerate, but you get the gist. It ends up where staff go off sick leaving the rest to carry the can, and then they get sick themselves – I do empathise with them really, it's just that when you are a patient it is hard.

Eventually I was sent to physio, and the physio took one look at my cording, rolled up her sleeves and set about 'popping them'. She showed me a way that I could sort of pull my skin taut, and then squish them till they popped, she seemed to enjoy doing it, and once I got the hang of it at home, I was well away, and I quite enjoyed popping them too.

Just two or three days post this op I was at a car boot sale. There's nothing in life that satisfies me as much as having a bloody good root around other people's junk, and huge bloody chest wounds were not going to stand in my way. High as a kite on morphine, I chatted to anyone and everyone – telling them the ins and outs of my surgery and doing the obligatory warning chat about not ignoring breast pain, my kids must be so bored hearing this over and over, but for a long time I was compelled to spread the word.

I bought some completely inappropriate clothes thinking they would 'help me feel good' when all was healed. They didn't. I recently went through the bag of clothes I'd bought that day– it was a sad jumble of 1990's prints, blazers with ¾ length sleeves that made me look like I'd shrunk it on a boil wash. A winter coat that had truly seen better days.

I wondered if I'd lost my mind at that car boot but remembered that I was off my face on morphine and after berating myself for wasting the more money I just had to park it. The clothes went to a charity shop and that was that.

Even the coolest of tailored jackets would have done nothing for me at that time – my tummy was still so distended from surgery, and now, piling in the cake because I felt I deserved it, thing were not going the right way.

Post double mastectomy, lifting any object with some weight to it was tricky. It was painful under my armpits where both wounds ended. I remember having to hold a travel mug of coffee with two hands to get it to my mouth at times. I had large swathes of numbness around my wounds – especially under the armpits, towards my back, and on my upper torso. Gradually over the months, the feeling came back. A good thing you would think – but with the sensation came a variety of electric shocks both day and night.

A lot of the healing seemed to be in line with the stinging and electric shocks, and for me this happened every day around the five-to-seven-month post-surgery. When I got roughly nine months post op – the pains woke me less frequently and the electric shocks diminished. I often puzzled over whether I felt like I'd been run over by a truck or seared with a hot knife.

Everyone was asking how I was, but I just didn't feel good, and didn't want to tell them about it. Some people wanted all the gory details, others just listened. My head was in a difficult place and nothing much helped except morphine and cake, but at least people had stopped doing that thing of calling me a warrior.

I spent the following seven months in considerable pain. Even if I could tolerate the pain by day – the pain at night woke me up, that stinging, searing pain, mostly on the site of the 'was healthy' breast. The right side was still exceptionally painful. So not only did I experience ongoing worries about death and dying, but catastrophic body image issues too, and I now had chronic severe pain to deal with – great.

I mostly put a brave face on it, at least in the daytime there were plenty of distractions. At night through – the stinging pain lasted months, it woke me in the night. I'd wake; not remember I had no boobs – then the pain, the trauma and a hell of a job getting back to sleep after that. I was tired by day but waking every night.

I had been warned I might get a phantom nipple but had already decided that no – I definitely wasn't.

By now, both my nipples had both been removed but I'd decided there was going to be nothing remotely phantom or weird happening about it thank you very much.

But it did. Damn.

I felt like a complete nut, I swear I could feel my nipple was there – not only that, it *was* itching – A LOT!

Apparently, it's common, and eventually it did go on its own, but I did spend a considerable amount of time itching nipples that were not there.

For a time, I walked around being far more acutely aware of my nipples than I would like. I could be being served at co-op, or filling up with petrol, it's a ridiculous thing that I'm talking to you, but thinking 'oh yes – my nipples have been cut off' – it's very distracting'.

To this day, one of the sweetest things that my son does, is that on the days my mobility is crap – he comes in to kiss *me* goodnight, and to protect my flat very exposed feeling chest, he *always* brings a big squishy teddy to cushion to protect my chest for our night night cuddle. In absence of boobs my flat chest feels sensitive, and I still wince at the idea of an elbow jab in the chest, so a big plushy teddy is the perfect barrier to cushion the sharp unexpected knocks, and it's so sweet that he still does this.

Other things I noticed post op, was that cuts and scratches took ages to heal, this was a real nuisance, as small scratches seemed to be getting infected, and insect bites sometimes took months to clear up. I put it down to the work my body was doing to focus on healing from all the surgery. I hadn't had antibiotics for ages, yet post op I seemed to be working my way through loads of them.

Other than that, memories were more around the daily struggles of life, trying to keep up with housework when your sleep is wrecked, and doing laundry when you can't carry heavy things is a nuisance. My daughter was a great help lifting baskets, but there were just so many times that I didn't want to ask her and had to use a carrier bag to move a few things at a time, it took ages, but I got there in the end.

Chapter 27
Lovely Doris

Doris and I continued to natter on the phone in the weeks following my op.

We were really excited about finally getting together and having a 'jolly good natter'. We were all ready to swap our life stories, to discover each other's back stories.

But it wasn't to be.

Just three weeks after my operation – Doris died, and I was devastated.

She had been my rock and now she was gone.

I'd missed the boat; I was just too long with my recovery.

I still feel that awful pain that we only narrowly missed that meet up as I write these three years on. How could I be *this* devastated about losing someone I barely knew.

I had managed to get to see her on her hospital ward just days before she died, I hobbled in in pain from my own op, I felt utterly selfish about the whole thing; she wasn't meant to die yet – we still had so much to say. I wanted to tell her how my op went, and she was going to tell me about her husband, her children, and her lovely cats. Selfish because I wanted our chat before she went.

But it wasn't going to happen – it was over.

I felt like my guts had been kicked, pulled out and kicked again.

I stood on the ward, whilst she was *only just* still alive, and just cried and cried and cried. I was devastated, just devastated.

The embarrassing thing was that some of her family were there, and they were very sad, but composed. They kept repeating, but Kate she's 93!

I felt like such a fool but was powerless to control my sobbing. I felt so traumatised it spoilt my last few minutes with Doris, I can't even remember what I said to her, I hadn't said what I'd wanted to say, I felt embarrassed because actual family were there – but there were things I'd wanted to say to her – yet I had the chance and didn't. I went home a complete mess.

I had to think about what the heck had happened, for me to cause such a scene, being so sad about someone I had known for just a few months.

I couldn't even attend Doris's wake a year on, because the sheer worry that I would *again* cause a massive scene which would be embarrassing and unbearable. What is wrong with me – why can't I control myself.

A year on, I still felt utterly traumatised about Doris, I was re-living the awfulness that we hadn't had that final meeting, and I just had to send my apologies – I just wouldn't be attending her wake. My apologies were accepted, and my panic subsided, but I was left with a lingering wonder about why I got in such a state about this.

I had a couple of hypotheses, which of course genuinely were around Doris being just lovely, and able to be present for me whereas many people around me were not, well not available to be there *in the way I needed* anyway.

I had come to rely on the stability of Doris and now she was gone.

She was a memory of that someone that came right out of the blue and into my life at *just the time I needed her* and then – poof, like a fairy godmother, as quick as she came, she was gone.

Chapter 28
The Pregnant Pigeon

After the op, I had to get used to strangers asking if I'm pregnant. People do stare at my physique – it's like a non-subtle second glance as if to say – there's something not quite right here – but they can't immediately work out what it is.

I had decided immediately post op that my physique now resembled a pregnant pigeon, and other people made me all the more aware of it. No matter how people try to hide it – without boobs their eyes automatically fall to my pregnant looking tummy. So frustrating as I am trying to fix it, but it remains a constant reminder that I look completely unbalanced minus my boobs.

This is a stand-alone chapter – because if you are considering having flat-closure mastectomy and you have an ample tummy – this could become a big thing for you too.

I am trying to reduce my weight, and for now I wear tummy control knickers when I'm out if I am feeling self-conscious just to balance my profile out a bit.

Chapter 29

Investigations

The initial euphoria of the first operation to remove the cancer had long waned, and I became tired of feeling triumphant at my 'light dusting' of cancer that had now gone.

This morphed into a chronic worry that cancer had returned to other parts of my body.

A relentless shape-shifting health anxiety which will put your GP surgery under a strain of fast-tracked investigations whilst you get to the bottom of it.

To date, I have had a bone scan of my ribs due to severe pain (we later established it was some of my cording popping that caused it).

I have had a hysteroscopy, colonoscopy, a plethora of blood tests, scans of my wounds, a second lot of ultrasounds on my ribs for three bizarre patches of redness. For this reason, I have become a *harder* person, not hard, but *tougher*, as the process of investigations, particularly the waiting for results repeatedly adds trauma to an already traumatised brain.

As I write this, I'm about to have a second hysteroscopy – all for mentioning that I had just two post-menopausal bleeds. I'm unbelievably grateful to my wonderfully proactive GP surgery, but it's just like – 'not again, can I not just have one month without instruments invading every orifice. I thought childbirth was undignified – but this is something else.

By now, my doctor's surgery all knew us well, and my health anxiety was beginning to be a bit wearing. The staff were kind, they really were, but the unrelenting worry and responsibility of saving my own life in order to be there for my children was nerve wracking, painful and left me emotionally spent.

I had to stop feeling like everything needed checking out, as I was going to give myself a new cancer worrying about it, or with all the X rays.

I have, three years on, started to chill out about new cancers a bit, but it never seems to go completely, and I hear that it can be completely normal given the circumstances.

Chapter 30
Aromatase Inhibitors

Sometime after my first operation my surgeon put me on aromatase inhibitors. I would need to be on them for five years to reduce the chance of recurrence.

Aromatase inhibitors are the living death that no one understands.

This is complicated by the fact that I have thyroid issues which I am pretty sure, if I muddle up the time I take my thyroid meds – all my symptoms of tiredness seem to be worse. I mention this because it gets really hard to pick out which thing is doing what.

Anyway - back to aromatase inhibitors - They the drugs that are supposed to block my body from producing too much oestrogen, because oestrogen is the hormone that made my cancer grow.

Ironic that on them, I feel like death.

It sometimes feels to me that if it's not the cancer that gets you, it's the meds that *treat the cancer*, because for me, my battle with this particular medication is where my real trauma seemed to begin.

There is no way that I can help you to understand quite how shocking the side effects of these drugs are.

My first experience of them was that they wrecked my already crap mobility, the pain was just unbearable, and nobody really understood – why would they. I had hot flushes all over again, despite my finishing the menopause in 2019.

I went through a period of getting intermittent shooting pains in my knee so sharp you think you'd been tasered.

Other days I feel weighted, like my entire body has been filled with concrete.

Or for a change It feels like I'm being stabbed with little pins in the knee.

Or a progressive ache all day till it grinds you to a stiff halt. I've had pain so bad in bed that I wished I could levitate.

The medicine seems to take it in turns to hit a certain part of your body for a time, then you take a short break, and it comes back and attacks a different limb.

Sometimes my leg feels like a shish kebab because it feels like it's had a metal pole stabbed vertically, right through it the centre of it.

Other times, it mimics viral infections, causing me to spike temperatures and making me shiver whilst feeling roasting. How can I feel hot *and* cold at the same time?

You're so accustomed to feeling sweaty, achy and gross that you completely overlook when you have *do actually have a virus*.

Just a couple of weeks ago I soldiered on despite feeling 'virusy' and went on a day trip, I did feel terrible when I was out, by the time I was following my daughter around a fashion shop, I felt like death. It turned out the next day that I had a bacterial infection – yes thanks for that cancer, now these stupid meds mean I genuinely can't tell when I'm ill or not and push myself harder to keep going when I shouldn't.

That darn infection took me from my usual 30% energy to a paltry 7% energy – wow that was a difficult couple of weeks.

After six months of one aromatase inhibitors, it eventually bedded in, the side effects settled, and the pain subsided to nothing. I unfortunately then had to take a 'holiday' from it once – for the hysteroscopy, and when I restarted it – wow it was shockingly awful – again for at least four months, and then, it bedded in again and I was okay. And then it wasn't again – the hot flushes returned with a vengeance, and far more brutal than those of my actual menopause – they feel like an absolute joke when you're struggling to cope as it is, and to top it off - my sleep was *again* annihilated.

I found the hot flushes to be far worse than those experienced in my menopause – but I couldn't strip off any more than I already was. The indignity of your children seeing you and all your lower wobbly bits in just a vest and pants is heartbreaking.

I tried to protect my modesty sometimes by tucking in one muslin cloth for my front, and one across my bum just to cover the tops of my legs a bit – I must have looked quite bizarre. I'll add it to their book of trauma they can present to a therapist in years to come.

Many times, I woke, sat up and immediately experienced a hot flush and palpitations so vile I thought I was going to throw up.

Even contemplating one step to put my slippers on was unbearable.

The sweats come on so violently and so fast that it's a shock to see my face transform from normal to bright red in a flash, and the beads of sweat on my forehead are visible. When it is as bad as this, if I am able to nip in the shower I do, but obviously with a busy life – it's not always possible to do this and the fan just has to do.

I felt like a zombie every morning and felt half asleep by half past two.

Holding conversations took untold effort, my concentration was shot, and yet again the flushes made my right armpit stink – although I will say that my left armpit now doesn't work very well post mangling, so at least that's half the smell.

I can really empathise with why people decide against taking this medication, I managed once to get through the pain barrier and out the other side. All other attempts at managing these meds have subjected me to random hits of excruciating pain that simply takes your breath away, and it's hard to live like that.

My patience was severely tested when a storm hit and the entire overhanging strip of the roof just dripped off the side of my house piece by piece.

The rest of the roof was already sagging, we needed a new roof, so out came the credit card and a new roof was got. I kept the team of roofers in tea and hot sausage rolls that week – I enjoyed looking after them but wow the back and forth of my ever-stiffening legs took its toll by the end of the week – I was utterly EXHAUSTED. The constant wearing pain gets under your skin gradually, it's an energy drain and grinds away at your mood.

It's so disheartening to see your house descend into a stinky muddle when your energy is crap. It's impossible to have visitors when you're struggling to do the barest of minimum of feeding people and making sure they all have clean things to wear, let alone it's hard to get the energy together to look nice when you feel terrible. Not to mention that a whole section of your wardrobe becomes unusable if it is made of artificial fibres or has long sleeves.

The final straw with one aromatase inhibitor was when I had become so disabled I needed a wheelchair at a mall. Words can't do justice to the pain that would bring tears to anyone's eyes that this medicine can bring, and with that chronic disability that comes hand in hand. My left knee had become unbelievable stiff, there were times it was impossible to kneel – even on a soft bed, as it felt as if my knees just crunched like biscuits – yuk! It's _so_ painful.

Using a wheelchair wasn't new to me – I suffered horrendous 'pelvic girdle pain' from just eleven weeks pregnant with my first child, when I suddenly struggled to walk up stairs and carry anything at all as it triggered a pain so bad it took my breath away. At that time I had to move into the dining room and use commode, as it got so bad I couldn't make it up the stairs unless I crawled. Thankfully I improved after using a good physiotherapist, but I will say that my mobility has never been the same since, something that current NHS physio's won't acknowledge, as they just put it down to age related back pain, but I know it isn't as when problems flare up, I get a recurrence of symptoms suspiciously similar to what I endured in pregnancy, often fluctuations in hormones seem to affect this.

Car journeys can be a nightmare with joint pain; I find being seated for longer than an hour can leave me exiting the car so bandy legged it looks like I've had a good session with the husband. Even using the public bathrooms when I am out becomes a chore. If I'm wearing tummy control knickers I can hold up the queue no end as it takes a huge effort to yank those up in a hurry when your bones are sore. Even taking my socks off feels like I'm dislocating my ankles.

The meds were also making me forgetful, I did stupid things like open two car windows that I had been told on numerous occasions were broken, resulting in bribing the car mechanic with chocolates to open the door panel and somehow force it shut. It's a real nuisance when I do stuff like this, it wastes everyone's time and I feel daft afterwords. It's like my mind can only retain so much and it just discards the rest.

I had become completely unable to reach the back of my low kitchen units, especially a deep corner unit which must by now have a stash of museum-worthy food in the dark depths of it. To top it off – staff were feeling so sorry for me limping around charity shops they were starting to offer me discounts (I didn't take them).

Aromatase inhibitors bring about a constant state of flux – you can never tell whether they're going to give you a shocking day from hell or a reprieve. One minute I'd think they were the bees' knees – they were going to give me a chance at life and once finished, I could run for the hills. The next day they would crush me, and I'd start thinking we need a bungalow, and if I was going to get to the top of any hill – I was going to need a stairlift to do it.

Pain is a real nuisance – it can make you into a complete misery guts and no wonder – who can go about their daily business against a backdrop of grinding stiffness and agonising pain.

My patience was tested, and occasionally it was a big fat fail.

To top things off, if you keep asking your doctor for codeine they will think you're addict. (I know, I know, I said I liked the morphine – but beyond that I'm quite happy without this crap in my system). It took no time for my card to be marked, and the request for codeine got increasingly difficult. (quite rightly so). Best to save yourself the humiliation of being treated like an addict as this does nothing to help your already in-your-boots morale.

(I don't want to give you the wrong idea though – I don't use drugs illegally and any mention of enjoying pain meds in this book is just honesty about enjoying the effects incidentally seeing as I needed to take them anyway).

I tried a different aromatase inhibitor, and that fooled me into thinking that it might be an easier ride.

Mild to moderate stiffness for about three weeks, then BOOM – a knackered right knee in the space of 24 hours. Gutted, just absolutely gutted.

My previously good right leg insidiously started to stiffen culminated in the grand performance overnight of ringing out with such pain you'd have thought a truck had run over it. By the following morning, I was OUT. I did not want this crap in my system ANYMORE and it was time for its eviction.

I could no longer live like this, couldn't even call it living – this was an absolute misery. I immediately stopped the meds and took a break for a few days.

After a bit of research online – I quickly realised that perhaps I should try it again, which is where I am at now, no side effects yet, but not holding my breath.

Sometimes I panic that life will always be like this, but hopefully it won't. The aromatase inhibitors will stop one day. Stopping and starting them feels like stalling a car, you sometimes just stop for a short time, but you do get going again.

The annoying thing about the pain waking you in the night, is that tiredness makes my pain worse, as does stress.

Surely the stress of living with such agony can't be good on the old cortisol levels.

The occasional self-imposed drug holiday reassures me that the pain is the meds and not a new cancer or sudden arthritis diagnosis. I don't take many breaks from these meds, but when I do I bask in the pain-free-ness of it all, and that lovely boost of a more normal energy in the afternoons, a welcome respite from feeling deceased by 3pm.

Sometimes I feel like switching things up a bit and play around with the time of day I take my meds– hmm, what shall I go for today – insomnia or feeling like my leg is on fire? Like some crap game of spin the wheel – but the options are all terrible – skewered thigh/biscuit knees/neck pain/foot pain/toe pain/wrist pain – the options are endless – what joy.

One last thing is to say that I have noticed my already thinning hair is thinning out even more since taking these meds, I've also noticed a few extra moustache and cheek hairs popping up, and also one in the middle of my neck!

Another thing is just prior to publishing – I'm pleased to say that I'm having a huge success since changing the time of day I take my aromatase inhibitors – I usually take it around 7pm or 8pm and it is going much better.

I still can get very tired 1pm onwards, but not always.

Contrary to my worry that taking these meds at night might keep me awake – I actually think I'm sleeping better now, making the most of that grogginess that they can bring hitting me at night.

My pain levels are minimal, I've been back to exercising and even for the first time in years managed a little slow jog for 10 minutes yesterday which I was very pleased about. I could not have done that on my previous aromatase inhibitor.

Interestingly, my first go at this new medication was horrifically painful, but after that short drug holiday I tried again and wow am I doing better now. I did have some severe pain and stiffness in my little finger over three nights, but that is all, and even that has now passed.

I have moaned like hell in this book about these meds – but at time of publishing I want to give you hope that *it is possible* to become pain free on them – it feels like luck of the draw, but whatever it is I'm grateful for the break I am having from severe pain, and I have truly made the most of it.

All those jobs that I used to look at previously, that I couldn't have even remotely contemplate - like deep cleaning the kitchen cupboards – I did yesterday with relative ease. Last week I reorganised the attic. Sometimes, it feels like you are stuck in agony on these meds forever, while your home descends into a dirty messy state and you can only look at it with sadness, but I'm living proof that sometimes – the pain isn't permanent, and even if it doesn't go away completely – you might be fortunate to enjoy some periods of time *pain free* and get a few bits done around the house.

Chapter 31

Doctor Google

Health Anxiety – ugh. Once you've been on the receiving end of bad news once, this is a tough one to manage.

Unfortunately – Aromatase inhibitors (although can be completely manageable for some), can also give you a plethora of side effects that give you actual symptoms of a new cancer – great!

The sweats I endured on aromatase inhibitors were next level – I spent months convinced that I had lymphoma, as a quick search on Dr Google kept telling me this. What made it worse was that I kept prodding my lymph nodes under my arm and in my groin to keep checking, which in the end was giving me *actual soreness* in those areas.

I contacted Dr Meadows, she reassured me that my bloods were fine, gave me a check over, and after that I just had to accept that they were a side effect from the hormone blockers.

The initial euphoria of having the cancer chopped out, was short lived. I soon realised that as soon as I got a new pain – I worried about it, and to make it worse – if I mentioned it to the GP – then they worried about it too.

What happened to the 1990's when doctors said things would *'probably be alright'* or *'watch and wait'*.

Now, doctors were investigating <u>everything</u> 'because of my history.

There's nothing more anxiety provoking than going to the doctor expecting some lovely false reassurance – only to see an ashen, panic stricken look on their face, followed by many focused questions and ending with a referral for yet another scan.

I was having so many scans to scan for cancer that I thought the scanners would actually end up giving me cancer anyway – was that even possible? – I will google it. Actually, no I won't.

I learned quickly to take a bit of 'reading that I'd been putting off' with me to the scan appointments, then at least I could do something useful whilst hanging around – sometimes for hours or even all day for that rib scan.

I once managed to read an entire very dry book that I'd been putting off whilst hanging around for a rib scan.

Even my foof itch was investigated.

As usual I got down to brass tacks in record time and discovered nurse calls hers a foof too. Did I have herpes? – apparently not.

Have you had sex with anyone other than your partner? She said,

'I don't think so' I said,

'You don't sound sure'.

'I have vivid dreams' I said, so vivid I get muddled at what I have and haven't done' I said. I barely knew what

day it was, and my anxiety had gotten so bad that I couldn't even be sure if my philanderous dreams were based on real life, I thought probably not, but I really wasn't sure.

Most of the GP's were fantastically understanding about my post-cancer health anxiety – all but one, who looked furious that I had the audacity to text in with *yet another cancer worry*. Her whole attitude was *off*, and it left me feeling like crap. I won't be seeing her again. I don't expect to be given the full range of tests when I present (again) with a new cancer concern – but I do, no matter how busy and burned out the GPs are – to be treated with dignity and respect. My own surgeon never treats me like this, she outright says that if I come to her talking of pains in various parts of my body – she will think 'cancer', it is her first thought.

Catching it early is the name of the game; we have to be careful what we pass off as *'probably nothing'*.

I kept thinking, that I had already found a 'hard to find' cancer once, so I wasn't going to give up easily. The frosty GP blamed my low energy on my bipolar and failed to validate that my waking ten times a night due to sweats and pain might eventually make me tired and peed off like anyone would under those circumstances. I haven't had a bipolar episode for years, so this was beyond annoying, it feels lazy, and like gaslighting me into my old diagnosis rather than looking at what is in front of her. I had to do some serious visualisation and meditation to disentangle my 'ness' from her yucky toxic crap.

I thought I'd better get my dental hygiene sorted too. I'd heard that bacteria in your mouth can cause endocarditis – and I definitely don't want that. I was surprised at the ease of which I got that appointment. I arrived at the dentist, but when the door was filthy and the carpet sticky and I became suspicious. By the time I was laid back in the dentist's chair I felt much more apprehensive, her bedside manner was akin to a barber surgeon.

I wouldn't have been at all surprised if she started trepanning my skull – except she wouldn't have, as she didn't have enough time, perhaps she was late for a train.

She knew what she was doing was hurting and did nothing to help me with it.

I made a wide range of painful noises, she stopped for a millisecond, looked 'on edge' and irritable that I was delaying her from her assault. She had the nerve to charge me for said mouth mangling – I should have charged her.

Note to self, if you're an adult in the UK and can *easily* get an NHS dental appointment – be very VERY suspicious indeed and always preload (with painkillers), I didn't and very much regretted it.

I recently saw an article where it described several symptoms of lung cancer – one of them was something to do with having finger clubbing. Since I had a dreadful cough and felt super poorly, I spent a week trying to work out if my fingers looked like spatulas thinking cancer may have returned, but the cough turned out to be a bacterial infection (which was pretty nasty actually), and fortunately the cough went away.

Another incident of concern was when I woke up recently to discover my foof was exuding 'eau de halibut'.

Not just for one day, for a few weeks : 0

I ignored it for some time, but when I was aware that the aroma was mildly permeating our bedroom, my anxiety peaked to full-on flap attack.

I wondered if I had a new cancer up my bits, I did feel sorry for myself – could nothing be spared? Whatever it was it couldn't possibly be good.

There was no ignoring it anymore, it was time to see the doc, so me and my niffy-nethers got ready and made our way again to the doctor's office.

Dr Meadows braced, and went in to check it all out, took a scraping for analysis and announced the results would be back in a few days. The results were all clear, and it turned out that the culprit was the tinned mackerel and peanuts I was eating for breakfast every day. Probably not the peanuts.

Incredible what such an innocent little tin of fish can do, but thank goodness that was all it was.

Chapter 32
An Obsession With Time

I developed quite an obsession with 'time' not long after my second op.

I had been trying to adopt an 'onwards and upwards momentum' and decided to take a razor-sharp look at exactly where I seem to 'lose' time.

I mentioned earlier that social media was the obvious one to check first.

I was shocked to discover a section of social media where you can monitor 'time spent' on the app. I was ashamed to discover that even on days where I thought I'd spent maybe an hour on social media – it could actually be more like two or three. What a monumental waste of time.

I used to be a regular poster on one app – but when I cast my eye back over what I was posting – it was mostly complete rubbish, which is even worse – cos then I'm wasting *other people's time* as well as my own. Initially it was great fun to get those validating 'pings' – but what for? Cancer shored up that realisation that if I just don't post in the first place – it saves other people from feeling like they 'ought' to 'like' my posts or feel *obliged* to comment if I've mentioned my kids or something about cancer – and then I wouldn't have to spend the remains of the day responding to the responses.

    I once wrote a vaguely funny post in the 'Extreme Dishwashers' group – it went nuts, my phones 'like' counter was going ninety to the dozen – a massive rush, but it glued me to the computer for a whole bloody day – what an utter waste of life.

Chapter 33
My Confidence Took A Hit

For the first time in our seventeen years of being together – I experienced pure panic at whether my husband might go off with someone else. He showed no signs of this, he is the kindest, most attentive and loyal person you could ever meet – yet I still had this panic.

It wasn't a constant thing – but it punctuated my lows in the cruellest of ways.

Whenever I hit a low, as mentioned earlier - I hit the cake equally hard. I was doing myself no favours but couldn't seem to stop myself from sliding ass backwards down that slippery slope of self-destruction, and since celebrating my 50th – the few wines that I was meant to have to celebrate the big day, soon turned into a regular thing.

Quickly I couldn't seem to get through the week without thinking Friday and Saturday nights should feel like a party. There did come a point when I decided enough was enough. Alcohol is well documented to increase chances of cancer returning, and much as it had once had its place as a crutch to cushion my worst days, its days were numbered and one day we agreed to stop buying it at all. I missed it for a couple of weeks but was surprised at how quickly I adapted to looking forward to a hot milk at bedtime instead, and hot milk to this day is still my favourite bedtime drink. I don't rule out having the odd glass of wine in future, but for now it has no place in my life. It's amazing what a couple of weeks break from alcohol can do in terms of getting your brain to switch focus to a different treat.

Chapter 34
I Thought I Was Supposed To Get Thin?

The breast care nurses were quite right, contrary to past notions that 'everyone who has cancer gets thin' – apparently quite a lot gain a bit of weight.

I certainly did that with knobs on. I found a photo of a fellow flattie, I knew nothing of her story, but there on google photos – was a stunning pic of her, with all her flatness stood proudly, and quite rightly so on a fashion catwalk. She has become a figure of hope to me, that photo alone – encourages me to become a healthier weight for me, which will – like her, help to balance out the thin top with a slimmer bottom. I will never look as good as her, not even close – she may even be young enough to be my daughter – but her beautiful photo is inspiring and gives me hope and something to aim for, and I sincerely thank her for that.

Chapter 35
Experimenting With What To Wear

I tried to buy tops with a bit of ruching or gathering across the neckline, but I just couldn't find what I was looking for. I then thought I'd try A line dresses. I saw a couple of new, floral A-line summer dresses second hand and ordered them. I thought that would work, slim dress at the top – but gradually tapers out at the bottom to disguise my bottom.

What actually arrived – were two bloody great floral parachutes. I don't care what anyone says – the dresses on those models were not the dresses that arrived.

So frustrated, I whipped out a needle and thread – and just started doing some fat running stitches across my plain supermarket round neck tops and gathering it up – hey presto, designer ruching on a budget top – well, not quite designer, but I was very pleased with the result. Because although I'm cool with my flatness – I still want to work on drawing the eye upwards to the neckline – so I often wear a necklace too, it seems to do the trick.

People keep telling me to get knitted knockers – *well you get* them I think – if you like them that much. I don't want two pin cushions attached to my frontage any more than I wanted my belly strapped to my front, but people do keep telling me about them. Don't get me wrong, the volunteers are incredible for making these – and they are wonderful, but it becomes another one of those things that random people tell you to get. When the whole point of becoming a flattie (for me) is to live flat – it just gets frustrating.

'I know', I think, yes – perhaps I *should* be having a monumental breakdown about not having two lumps of fat sticking out my front – but apart from certain moments - I mostly don't. Would I like my own lovely firm pert breasts back – yes, I would, but I really don't want anything that's been fashioned stuck to me thank you for your concern. It makes me feel like I can't possibly believe that I look acceptable with my ironing board flat chest.

Apart from a couple of impressively well contained patches of severe depression – I don't get all my ideas of attractiveness from having boobs or not.

I love chatting to people, love the rollercoaster of an interesting chat, and the highs of a cracking good belly laugh with someone you know well. My attractiveness, for me, comes from within, a feeling of confidence, that some people really enjoy my company – maybe not that many – but some, and I like those 'some' very much.

It is far more important to me that my body feels authentic *to me*, that I can feel where it 'begins and ends', and I don't have anything numb stuck to my front.

This is in no way a criticism of those who do have reconstruction – as I have already said – I have seen the work of my own surgeon on others – and the reconstructive results can and often do look stunning. It's just that we are all so different. If I could have accepted the numbness, or loss of sensation in reconstructed boobs – then great, but I just can't.

I once tried hair extensions, many years ago, but I couldn't even stand that. Overnight – one by one I picked each of the attached clumps of hair out of my hair and felt utter relief when they were in the bin. The hairdresser couldn't believe it. Something about me gets into a real state when I start attaching things that aren't meant to be there to myself – and that's what I have to go with.

Chapter 36
Other People's Perceptions – Feeling Invisible

Regarding my cancer, overall, three years on, folks are bored shitless, and who can blame them. I'm supposed to shut up about it now, but there's still a black cloud. When the drama ends no one is interested.

This journey has been a huge insight into how disability and trauma can leave you feeling completely invisible.

No one wants to hear about my physical or mental pain, that I'm struggling like hell to get around, I sometimes get into quite a panic state about my sudden loss of mobility – it can feel like beyond a two-minute mention of it they seem to awkwardly search for something supportive to say then want you to move on.

Beyond that initial drama of cancer, it's all a big yawn. It's a big yawn for me too, but the poop keeps coming and you feel like screaming long past the whole debacle – but like a nightmare and it feels like no one's hearing you.

In the beginning – my cancer news was (mostly) big news all round, but eventually lots of people must have tired of it, and I got fed up with repeating the same story over again myself. Sometimes I'd unexpectedly get the third degree, and I'd leave the conversation so violated and drained I'd have to go to bed – even in the middle of the day.

On reflection – and as always, people couldn't do right for doing wrong – they are not mind readers, they too have their own lives and struggles, and they could easily have been tired, in pain or just distracted, and were not able to be present with me no matter how much they wanted to be. It's easy to see this now, but at the time it felt like a real lottery as to what I was going to get.

Not saying I'm the most attractive of people at the best of times, but I can scrub up when I want to. It's interesting to see when guys are looking at me, to catch that glimpse of my chest that they think they discreetly do, and then a moment of confusion.

Not saying at all that all people who love boobs are idiots – but I do class my flatness as a well-functioning idiot filter.

If anything happened to my husband – I would be devastated, I can't imagine ever finding anyone as lovely as him, and for that reason and many others, I just wouldn't want to be with anyone else.

The fact that I'm flat as a pancake now gives me confidence that it might stop some from trying. Prior to marriage – I was fiercely independent and very happy to be single for much of my life, I've been blessed with the most compassionate caring husband, but beyond that I'm absolutely not interested. I love my children, I love my books, I love my pets and that is plenty enough for the rest of my life thank you very much.

I'm long past strangers fiddling with my parts, and having no boobies has served as an insurance policy to prevent unwanted attention. You can see their minds ticking over wondering if they did bang me – where would they put their hands and I can't help feeling mildly amused.

Chapter 37

Competition Of Who's Had The Worst Health Problems

Me talking about cancer engendered all manner of other people seeing fit to blast me with their health issues as a reply. It became a competition of who'd suffered the most, who had the goriest surgery, who had had the most invasive investigations – until one day I was out.

Enough was enough, I couldn't do this crap anymore – what were we doing? – This isn't a conversation – it's some kind of bizarre symptom exchange. It's not that I'm not interested in other people's health, it's that a discreet few people latch on to my operations and start competing about who had it the worst. I now try to avoid mentioning anything that will leave me wide open to this, as much as possible I say nothing.

Chatting about health between my nearest and dearest is no issue – we are there to support each other – it's the ones who take it to competitive extremes that I get tired of.

Chapter 38
Who Is For You? Who Is Against You?

My inner circle consists of close family and a handful of friends that I have had for years – people who have close access are firm supporters, great listeners and most of all are very encouraging when it comes to supporting my hobbies or dreams.

I do however pride myself on having an incredible poop-detector. I've tweaked its settings until I can now smell a narcissist from one flash of a facial expression. I've studied the work of prominent psychologists and learning as much as I can about this has created results in my life have been staggering – a painstakingly curated inner circle of people who have my back.

Who fills your cup – who drains it?

This is the rigorous test I put everyone through in order to decide if I need to adjust the current level of access they have to me, my information, my life.

As mentioned earlier - updates in the wrong hands becomes supply – I'm not a petrol station that's there to top up people's low self-esteem. Friendships I enjoy are mutually supportive, not a squirrelling away of someone's bad news in order to fill up your own cup.

I'd already been warned about people feeling envy when you share great news, or the flash of joy when you tell them something really unlucky happened to you– it ticks me off. Worse is the elusive – texting them positive news – you did something good; you achieved something, you challenged yourself – and what do you get? – a big fat nothing = red flag.

Your good mates will cheer you, will say well done when you try and pat you on the back for giving it a go. Give a narc the option of good or bad news and they'll crack out the popcorn and take the bad every single time. I was already clued up to this stuff, but cancer gave me a razor-sharp focus to weed people out that were doing this crap. I had discovered quite how short life was, and no longer would these people have close access.

Chapter 39

Who Did I Let Go Of And Who Did I Gather Up For The Journey Onwards?

Some people took great interest when I was struggling but disappeared the minute I got myself together – unable to cheer me on for grabbing life by the horns, galloping forwards – they just fell to the wayside, and I didn't look back.

How can you *not be* pleased that someone is feeling mentally and physically better post-cancer, and that they are making positive steps to shape an exciting future – I just don't get it.

I already knew about the secondary gains that can be used from taking on the role of being 'sick' but had never experienced that someone would gain from another person being the poorly one – and subsequently feeling challenged when that person moved on.

I'd rather have infrequent contact with a quality friend than regular contact with a frenemy. I aim for a high-quality friend that's a good listener, positive about the future and encouraging of others to attain their goals. I will tolerate *intense loneliness* in place of fake and sub-par – I have plenty of hobbies and would rather spend time with those than sat next to someone that is not *for* me.

I try to be a good listener – but if it's starting to be a broken record – and I'm smelling that repetitive whiff of 'eau de tragedy' I do have to have a really good think.

Another thing that gets my goat is when people attempt to go all 'parental' on me and start treating me like a child. I spot this in milliseconds, I dislike it intensely, and anyone speaking to me like this has marked their own cards.

I see it a adjusting my equalizers, or volumes – I turn some people up, others down and just mute the rest.

People who wander around in a permanent state of 'fury' also get on my tits – that doesn't really work does it – anyway, the only people I like who are permanently furious are Jackdaws – who manage to exude the exquisite balance of a look of both derangement and fury.

I heard someone say how seductive and energising rage is. There are people who just love nothing more than moaning and being outraged. They hang onto your every word waiting for the negative bits – if the negativity isn't forthcoming, they are left hanging in a state of impotence, frustrated and disappointed.

I initially felt lonely when I stopped posting on social media – because despite handing out your email on the way out – no one cares what you're doing once you uninstall it. And why should they – if you're not on there smoothing *them* – why should they smooth *you*. It all felt silly, soul-less and a big waste of time, so now I fill my head with books and that seems to be going better.

I don't for one minute think that this would suit everyone – but it's personal to me that cancer really forced me to focus on those that matter, who really is cheering my corner? Who has my back? Who would throw me under the bus? Who asked how I was post op – not that many, and I don't ask much about the wider circle either – so as said previously, I totally deserve the ambivalence I got.

To me, a good friend is also someone I can message, without frantically worrying after - that I've said the wrong thing.

Most of all in life, I don't actually want someone to constantly moan at, cancer came to me, and why not? – why shouldn't it be me – I smoked, drank but above all it could have arrived in a totally random way or just a few cells in my body that were ticking time bombs anyway. Whichever way – I had it, but onwards and upwards and I much prefer planning positive stuff than I do moaning about stuff – yet people inevitably seem to want to hear the negative stuff and not the positive.

Some of the most stellar support came from some of the most unexpected places.

Some people were struggling with the most significant mental health issues themselves – but were still able to be generous with their time, and through their own suffering – were the kindest supporters despite having the least reserves in terms of coping with their own life. It felt akin to the poorest mate you have, who has barely anything in her cupboards but still feeds you up when you only nipped in for a brew.

Chapter 40
Listening To Others' Problems In The Early Days Can Be Hard

I really struggled with people offloading their problems too much when I was mid-surgeries – I just did not have the bandwidth to deal with it – particularly when they're making no attempt to deal with it themselves.

I wanted to say – 'the agony aunt has shut shop'. I'm afraid she shut up shop July 22 when a cancerous lump erupted out of her chest. Or an out of office reply saying – Kate's currently fighting for her life, she'll be back when she's good and ready – in the meantime feel free to get yourself some counselling.

I got really peed off with people continually messing up my peace. Within a couple of months, I ditched most social media and developed a new North Star of protecting my peace and holding my power. A seismic shift of bulldozing a-holes out of my life was freeing, empowering and most importantly - it felt good.

I decided to focus instead on the few genuine people in my life – focus my energy on them instead, and with this in mind I started to put real effort into those people.

There was one issue with this though, which was whereas my inner circle of friends had been used to a certain level of contact, when I suddenly upped my interest in them a few may have been perplexed at the sudden influx of extra attention. I had not updated them that I'd binned off everyone who *didn't have my back* and was now diverting that previously wasted energy into them. I lavished long emails and lengthy podcast worthy voice notes on them – but it was too much. I felt that I had been mistaken in throwing so much attention their way – these people had busy lives, so I made the decision to calm the heck down and try to be normal again, and soon enough, there was once again a feeling of equilibrium.

Chapter 41

Sex Life

Now here was a challenge. I needed to prove to myself that my sex life wasn't over pretty soon after surgery. Surely the lack of boobs can't be a deal-breaker, can it? Fortunately, I bagged an incredibly supportive husband who assured me that apart from what I do to my chest is my business alone, if I did go ahead with surgery, then he would hugely appreciate that I may just be able to be around longer, far more than any joy a perky set of boobs.

I decided that finding a focus away from it all being 'on me' – seemed to be the way to go. Popping on a *romantic* movie, really seemed to help. I also discovered a clothing brand which makes lacy underwear especially for women who have flat-closure mastectomies. The underwear is absolutely gorgeous and could really help some people if it is something they are self-conscious about. Just wearing a pretty bra-top was enough to cover my sore bits which may have distracted both of us from the more sensual moments.

I will say politely that post-mastectomy - the peak of romantic moments can cause your fresh breast wound to sting in the strangest fizzy unpleasant way! – those nerves are very sensitive to *dramatic moments* – fizzy-tit-sting be warned!

Chapter 42

Operation Number Three

I was fine with being flat, but being deformed was not cool. My surgeon had done an incredibly neat job of the two lines across my chest, but I still had managed to have the result of *having a cleavage*, but no boobs : 0

If I lay on my side or leaned forward my stand-alone cleavage was obvious, and to me it was an embarrassing reminder of how disfigured I was. This isn't anything that my surgeon did wrong, this is my body doing what it wanted to after healing.

Whatever it was, it needed to be gone. I cannot be having an ample and seductive cleavage but no tits. No, no, no, that is not going to work at all. I spoke to my surgeon and an operation to remove my cleavage and dog-ears was arranged.

If I was to have any hope of mentally fully accepting my appearance. It was ruining my silhouette and making it impossible to wear a vest – which feels like a catastrophe when you're having evil hormone blocker hot flushes.

For these reasons, I was glad to be having this op, it was a last-minute cancellation – and I was <u>very</u> grateful.

The usual questions cycled round my brain – why am I doing this/what if I get sepsis/what if I die on the table? Except it feels all the more unnecessary when it's an op purely to *tidy you up*. I would feel like a real wally if I died on the table in the name of removing my 'dog ears'. Mind you – those dog ears were ultra puffy and really rubbed in the summer, that seemed enough of a reason alone to chop them off.

It was a rude awakening, as at the final hour, I learned that I was first on the list for surgery, so the kids had to be hauled out of bed early to get me to the ward. I had to get up ridiculously early in order to go for a poop.

My bowels are rigid in their routine – they like me to be up and about for some time before they get going – it was a real nuisance, as I could have done with the extra sleep. I'd learned by my mistake previously – as I had not had my morning evacuation for op one – I thought I could trick my bowels into bypassing the 'need to go' until post op – but oh no – they were fired up and ready for action just at the moment the entire theatre were smiling, gloved up and ready to go. I felt especially stupid as I'd already caused the whole 'orange-juice gate' debacle, only to then make the entire surgical team have to wait whilst I evacuated my bowels – not easy when the stressed frosty nurse was banging on the loo door to hurry me up.

I arrived at the ward, a staff nurse went through the forms, and asked if I was under 55 – knock *me when I'm down* why don't you – nothing wrong with being 55, but I'm not quite there yet nursie.

My surgeon checked me over – I felt bad for having gained weight pre op, which was likely to spoil the result. I asked if I'd spoiled the likely results much and she kindly said not at all, but I knew really that the end result was not going to look great given my weight gain. I was furious with the idiots who tipped me into unnecessary stress, that caused this.

This is where the stress people dump on you has real tangible results in the form of poor surgical outcome – my results were not going to be nearly as good as they could have been if it wasn't for certain people bringing crap to my door. Some people do not seem to realise or care about the impact of the stress they cause you, and I find this hugely unjustified and frustrating.

The anesthetist did his final checks – he looked so much like one of my kinky ex-boyfriends who used to encourage that I went to the gym because *'I was carrying a bit extra'* the cheeky git. I used to nickname him 'pervert-boy' (not in a good way 'cos he got right on my nerves) and I dumped him pretty quick for wasting our money at lap dancing clubs then lying about it – ooh he was a git. Thankfully I managed not to declare any of this to the anesthetist[4].

---

[4] My OCD tells me I definitely *did* declare all of this and more to the anesthetist whilst semi-conscious – thanks OCD – but I don't think I did – (we'll have this out in private).

The nurse came to see me moments before being wheeled off, she commented on the state of my *messy* hospital table.

I had somehow managed to create that doom-pile-esque vibe in a 'home from home' kind of way – piles of tissues, pens, wipes, books, magazines and snacks.

It reminded me of a budget hotel cleaner many years ago commenting on the piles of stuff in our hotel room – hands to the face she entered the room and shrieked in horror and declared she'd *'rather commit suicide than sleep in this room'*. She couldn't understand why we had brought our own dvd player, a selection of dvds, a buffet of instant snacks and our own body-weight in drinks. There was not an inch of table left visible in that hotel room as we were mightily well prepared.

Anyway, back to the op - apparently – my tidy up operation lasted ninety-five minutes.

I made a note in my little book to say that in recovery, *I spent thirty minutes looking at my slippers and the call bell, not being able to reach either, I spent the entire time wondering how long it would take for someone to come by.*

Over the course of the three operations – the pain does kind of decrease somewhat – as eventually – everything is *so mangled* that your body just feels numb.

When I was finally able to mobilise – I was aghast to see my pillow and bed sheets splashed with yellowy liquid – was this *fat-splash*?

Is liposuction that messy that it sprays the bed? I didn't complain about it; I was lucky enough to get this op, so I certainly wasn't going to complain about some mere fat-splash.

Uncanny in hindsight though – how I seem destined to come out of surgery to find parts of myself on the bed, as in the first op it had been a lump of tit, and here now I was faced with the look of my own fat.

As I lay in my bed – I thought that calling this a mere 'cosmetic tidy up' didn't do justice to what had just occurred. It had been ninety-five minutes of the kind surgeon, using a combination of years of skill and a good dose of elbow grease to hoover my fat up a steel pipe then close me up in such a way that I look as neat as possible.

As with all my ops, shopping was the thing I most wanted to do on discharge, so I insisted on stopping off at a clothes shop on the way home – I can't remember what it was now – probably a nightie or something – but I do remember making a concerted effort *not to be incontinent* in the shop – the anesthetic does weird things to your continence. Yet again – I looked like I'd escaped from the psyche-ward, yet again I cared not.

I was allowed to take my bandages off *way sooner* than I was prepared for – even allowing the shower to cascade over my frontage terrified me. As with all three ops I dreaded removing my bandages. I could have quite happily gone through the rest of my life bandages left on – I was not keen at all to see what gory mess lurked under there – no thanks.

I remember being worried about taking my bandages off as my armpit hairs got trapped in them, and I hadn't shaved because of my removed lymph nodes. As is often the case, post-surgery I lost a day, so the bandage coming off came sooner than expected.

A compromise post-bandage was to always wear a fresh new cotton vest every day – that way I could pop it on before I get to the mirror keeping my delicate self-esteem vaguely intact.

A week and a half post op – I took my dressings off and had approximately 3-4 inches of wounds each side. The appearance of my chest seemed like someone had being doing one of those dot-to-dot puzzles on it – as if they've put some little anchoring stitches here and there to stop it all going skew-whiff.

After examining my wounds I felt a bit queer, was sporting a mild fever so took to my bed.

Incidentally, I had been wheeled in for op three in excruciating mobility pain, the sort that is so bad it takes your breath away – only to emerge pain free in my legs – what a joyous moment that was – a reprieve from that constant pain. I wondered if during surgery something had been disrupted in my legs when they were hauling me around – I did not care – it was wonderful. However, I did subsequently have a searing back pain which rendered me star shaped for ninety-five minutes.

The reprieve from leg pain was, however, short-lived. It returned with a vengeance after two weeks – back to wondering if a bungalow would be better – and searching for walking sticks online.

I also had sore lips, and a dry throat, but at least I didn't feel sick – hallelujah.

A common theme post op was to feel very anxious about all the lumps and bumps along the line of my fresh wounds. There seemed to have been much folding of my skin by the surgeon whenever he closed me up at the end of an op, I was at times alarmed at the thickness of what felt like half am uncooked pasty under the wounds, and lumps on the chest is not what you want to feel at any stage of the game. In time – these bulky lumps seemed to somehow disappear into nothing.

I had really noticeable nipple pain after all three ops.

Given I had no nipples at all – this was still very strange.

After op three I remember wondering about feeling a sting in my nipple area – which was odd – as I had not had nipples for eighteen months. I'm guessing the nerves that used to supply my nipples had been mangled yet again, it subsided after time but was mildly disturbing for a bit – it kind of felt like my nipples were gripped by a G clamp and again was a distraction throughout many conversations with people, but thankfully I didn't mention it.

One saving grace was that I was able to shower my bottom half - if I was careful – this was sheer bliss! Next best thing to a shower was running water as hot as I could take it, on a flannel, and strip washing my top half. It was the same joy you get when air stewards pass you a steaming hot flannel at the end of a long flight – lovely!

Being in bed at home post op was a disaster for my mobility – I quickly became weak again, which was a nightmare for reaching into far corner spaces to clean - it was not unusual for my back to go into spasm and I'd be stiff as a board for the day – back to be on anti-inflammatories and codeine.

I was given post-op physio exercises to do I like to think I did everything by the book post all of these ops, but I clearly didn't – as I drank banned substances prior to my first and most lifesaving op, almost derailing it, but getting back the exercises that are there to prevent lymphedema – I had a go after the first op, but I got a bit bored with them after the second op and by the third – there was a period of time where If my arms blew up like elephant legs it would have been entirely my fault. I wonder how many people actually do their exercises properly, and how many admit to their physio that they didn't.

This time, I had shooting pains after ten days, and surgery three is still stinging on one side six months later. I have been doing light weights recently, and I do bingo wing exercises where you have both arms outstretched behind your back, holding weights and lifting them *just slightly* fifty times, only with weights I fear I have disrupted some of the healing, as I'm now getting strange stinging pains on my right wound site.

At time of writing, I am waiting to be seen by my surgeon to double check that a new cancer hasn't sprung up on the healthy side, best to check it out as *stranger things have happened*, although staff in the breast team have assured me that the sound of this wound pain six months post-op still sounds in the range of normal – I'm pretty sure it was my bingo wings exercises disrupting the healing which caused this pain, because now that I have stopped doing them the pain has gone away. Just goes to show that you can still disrupt all that healing that you can't see under the skin months after the operation.

Chapter 43

Post Surgery Number Three

With a fleshy goiter, varicose veins, wildly out of control thrush and continence to rival a hamster I'm not feeling quite so attractive.

I hold out hope of looking good in a sharp little jacket. I've had my hair done, and bought a few bits of makeup, I'm gradually reducing weight so I can match my bottom to my top – it will be a long process – but it's all going in the right direction.

Surgery three added the excitement of not just physical disability and mental trauma – but a unique look of being cut across the chest 'ear to ear' – I looked like I'd been put through with a pencil sharpener. It was impossible to wash my hair, and I had that post-surgical oil-slick look – I discovered it's hard to put your hair up when it's clumped together.

Now being able to style my oil-slick with a spatula, combined with a monumental dirty incident involving a blocked loo and a toilet brush – I decided it was time to bite the bullet and wash my hair against all medical advice.

I washed my fine split hair with the shampoo equivalent of washing up liquid – it's a luminous green liquid created to degrease the oiliest of mops.

It was wonderful to get right in there and shampoo out that nasty grease. Until it came to get a brush through it. My frizzy flyaway hair had merged into a big pet burr only seen on animal welfare videos highlighting a tragic rescue. Now I was going to have to attend hospital looking like an abused dog in need of a trip to a dog grooming parlour. In the end after much panic – I applied the equivalent of a chip pan's worth of oily frizz serum back onto it and was once again able to style it with said spatula – Same result, though less stinky.

As warned – despite wearing a bin bag in the shower - my yellow rubbery bandages got wet resulting in alarming squelchy noises with every footstep. Convinced this was now some version of a squelchy-sepsis or fungi, or maybe an apocalyptic wound collapse – I was most pleased that in just four hours I was due for a wound check at the hospital. I was delighted to pre-load (with painkillers) for this, which calmed my mental state somewhat.

I arrived at the hospital – the kind nurse gently removed the fat yellow dressings, waltzed out of the room to find my surgeon, leaving me with what I can only describe as the smell of *mortuary bums dressed with honey* – a strange yet pungent aroma radiating from my frontage – this was the smell of infection surely – but apparently not – it's just the smell of healing wounds and rubbery strange dressings. The nurse patted away at my wounds for which

I did not feel ready for, nevertheless, it's always good not to have apocalyptic wound collapse, so I went home and breathed a sigh of relief.

Chapter 44
Phoenix Rising (Hopefully)

I decided to draw a line under the whole poop show and challenge myself to do something out of my comfort zone. So, for my 50'th, I attended a huge writing event on my own. I missed my husband and children, but the date coinciding with my 50'th, felt like it was meant to be - something I just had to do, to mark my next steps forward post cancer.

At this time, I had not been drinking alcohol for ages, but the offer of free bubbly coming around on trays was all too much, and I did indulge. Fortunately, I managed to get my husband to pick me up before descending into full on mental diarrhoea.

I had started to deteriorate as I was aware of waffling to writers, so I was extra glad when my husband had arrived, and I could be removed to a place safe from causing myself any embarrassment.

I love the idea of challenging the heck out of yourself, getting out of your comfort zone and spreading your wings, hopefully I can create more opportunities to do this in future, as it keeps me on my toes.

Chapter 45
Tips To Manage Aromatase Inhibitors

The suggestions that follow are a real mish-mash of ideas I picked up online at the beginning of my journey, with a couple of my own thrown in for good measure.

<u>Gel Pillows</u> are now an essential part of my life, I ordered them online, and I just love them so much – instant relief when I'm sat or lying down from those awful hot flushes. I don't put mine in the fridge – I just have a few lined up for the night, and when I've warmed up the current one, I fling it out (occasionally they land on my husband's head by mistake), and I swap it for a cool one. Amazing how quickly they absorb our heat too.

I also couldn't manage without my <u>USB fan</u> with five speeds. I use a 'round the neck fan' daily, it's much more convenient that I can just walk around with it blowing cool air towards my ears.

If I'm really struggling on hot days – then I whip out good old fashioned <u>muslin cloths</u>, wet them under the tap and lay those out over me like a sheet – works better if I'm able to take a brief water shower and just not dry myself properly, but obviously I can't shower five times a night, so the wet muslin cloth works just fine.

I also bit the bullet and bought a <u>shopping trolley</u> for when I'm out and about, as the smallest of weight to carry like a drink can really take it's toll if the aromatase inhibitors are causing pain problems. Being able to pop my shopping in the trolley far outweighs any worries I used to have about them not being for younger people – honestly, when I'm shopping, who cares.

<u>Intermittent rest</u>, when cooking – if you put a chair by the cooker so you can take the pressure off your legs – even for just a minute or two can just eek out your mobility to get you to the end of tea.

I <u>sit to chop veg</u> sometimes; it is that thing of why stand if you can sit. I was surprised to discover that using a salad spinner hurts post op – it feels really weird and a bit icky after a mastectomy.

Having a selection of <u>brushed cotton</u> and cool cotton bedding was a life saver for the changes in season too.

If you're able to <u>ask another human to wash up/or load the dishwasher</u> for you – you can take that well-earned – end of the day hot shower, and rest in bed with a hot water bottle under your sore leg. That way – the following day you have a better chance of your body resetting and you can do it all over again.

<u>Heated knee thing</u> – I ordered a heated knee pad, that seemed to help some days for the extreme knee pain.

<u>Distraction</u> – <u>audiobooks</u> saved my life so many times, I discovered that distraction markedly helped with the pain. Whenever my book stopped, I could quickly hear my legs shout at the pain they were in, it just got louder and louder until I popped a new book on and got lost in that.

Other forms of distraction that worked for me – were studying up on writing – I made use of these times to buy some courses online that I could do at home. I've often felt like I could do with a stint in prison to get some reading done – instead, I got cancer, but I made use of the time, nonetheless.

Christmas movies, motivational videos (ad free if poss.) and reading dusty old literature books also worked for me. I couldn't deal with watching anything too scary – hence Christmas movies and classic literature was plenty to get my teeth into. I wanted to watch some good old fashioned 90's movies, but the cost of buying movies online seems to have ratcheted up, so I dug out the old boxes of DVD's and dusted them off and then embarked on a mission to curate my own video library via the charity shops. DVDs used to be ten quid back in the day – now they are ten for a quid! How times change. I now have a fab 'library' of films, where I can guarantee that there will be something in there to suit my very mood at any given time.[5]

---

[5] I will say however, that until I squirrelled these bargains away – they were contributing massively to the doom-pile vibe in our house, and if we ever had any notions about selling up – these bloody great towers of DVDs were going to create the 'wow factor' – for all the wrong reasons.

I got the sense that some people around me were unimpressed about what I was spending on educational courses, but it's nobody else's business what we spend our money on, and they are courses to improve my family's quality of life and earning potential – not handbags! (and if you want to buy yourself a handbag there's nothing blooming wrong with that anyway x).

Hobbies or any distraction can serve as great pain relief. I rarely feel pain when I am writing, once I get in a flow state it's not unusual for me to remain pain free throughout the whole time.

I tried at times to use these grey spaces of hanging around for appointments or dull drawn-out recovery times to feather my cap with something. However small the feather was, it felt like my life was improving in small steps. It helps your confidence when you get to the end of the year and think well that was a challenging year – but at least I managed to learn X, Y and Z.

Managing aromatase inhibitors became a combination of everyday exercises to strengthen my legs and core muscles – this helped a lot. I was then able to utilise intermittent bed rest to do my own admin, like calls to school/doctors/dentist etc. No point doing these calls standing up if I don't have to.

Even sat upright in a chair made my mobility so much worse – so it really was the short bursts of horizontal rest that made a difference.

On days my legs were doing better – I'd use that chair for intermittent rest and also intermittent sit to stand exercises whilst my rice was bubbling away – strengthening my legs at any opportunity made all the difference.

Something about not overestimating your ability to stay standing by teatime, if you have a few foods as back up then you're well covered, and less disheartened.

Chapter 46
Write Your Meds Down

I've lost count of the times I had a box of painkillers in my hand, got chatting and then couldn't remember if I'd taken them or not. This was a real nuisance when managing the side effects of aromatase inhibitors, speaking of which I keep forgetting if I've taken those or not too – I need to mindfully take them as I am sure I have ended up doubling the dose by mistake a couple of times.

Nowadays I have to focus like a nurse on a meds-round when administering my own meds and writing them down helps me pace them, so I have better cover throughout the day.

I ought to add (re aromatase inhibitors pain), that prior to exercising – standard painkillers like anti-inflammatories and paracetamol barely touched the surface, I found codeine helped to a point, until my pain then found a way to override the codeine and other meds to shout so loud about the pain that I'd got into a real muddle.

As mentioned earlier the doctors were understandably not keen to keep dishing out opiates, so I decided to stop aromatase inhibitors, decrease my pain, embark on a period of training in readiness to try a new aromatase inhibitor. With the start of the new aromatase inhibitor post-exercise – my stronger body seemed to respond better to anti-inflammatories and paracetamol again – it was almost as if I'd had a reset button and could try again.

Once, my husband brought me some peanuts in a little bowl, which had a spoon with the two anti-inflammatories I'd requested perched neatly on it. Unfortunately, I was watching telly, grabbed the bowl and mindlessly shoveled the painkillers into my mouth thinking they were peanuts and crunched them – yuk! – don't do this! – painkillers taste GROSS! They're kind of peppery and vile. I was traumatised by this for some time before I was able to take them again – I even felt iffy about eating peanuts for ages.

Get housework/DIY jobs done in those little gaps between aromatase inhibitors – you might be able to get a few jobs done. I could be completely disabled for weeks – take a break from aromatase inhibitors – then manage quite well to gut a storage unit/reorganise our attic/do a massive de clutter/reorganise the garage.

I'm not encouraging you to take breaks so that you can get jobs done, more to make the most of a natural break if you are having to take it under medical advice.

Aromatase inhibitors seem to be hell bent on making me out to be a liar and an idiot – one minute I was hobbling like I've just crawled out of a grave, the next minute I was zipping around charity shops like an easter bunny – I swear some people stopped talking to me thinking I talk rubbish because of this. I honestly felt at times that my own meds were mocking me.

Chapter 47
Would I Recommend Flat Closure Mastectomy?

No.

I would recommend not getting cancer in the first place.

If I could have tolerated the reconstruction – that would have been a brilliant option.

The days I spend wondering how flat my tummy could have been if I'd had reconstruction, and how much better all of my clothes would look – but I knew in my heart of hearts that I would not be able to tolerate the worry that I might not be able to spot a new cancer.

Maybe it was partly because my cancer had been deep under the nipple, all the medics kept saying how lucky I was to find it, so now I feel left with no option but to give myself the best possible chance of noticing any further issues.

Having reconstruction – for me, would feel like placing a cushion over my chest and never letting me look to see what was occurring underneath – it just wasn't for me.

Flat closure was a last resort.

It doesn't fully remove the worry of cancer though. My worry about breast cancer *is* dramatically reduced, but it is not by any means gone completely.

You can still get breast cancer on the chest wall, or on the underside of your breast skin. I regularly check for lumps and bumps by mimicking the finger walking along the straight scars I have – but even now, despite being flat as a pancake, I can still get quite worried about the slightest of bumps.

I was never going to be the sort of person to cope with a lumpectomy, or even just a single mastectomy – so this option suits me better but is by no means perfect in terms of self-reassurance – and that feels like almost a tragedy at times, because after everything I've put my body through, and the psychological trauma, I still worry to this day about the dreaded recurrence – so what was the point.

If you have doubts about whether you feel mentally strong and resilient enough to cope with how your body image is post-op, I would seriously think about whether this is the right option for you.

If, after going flat, you feel so depressed about your body image, which could affect your sex life, your confidence in public, it could even affect your relationship with your partner – It could create a huge set of problems for years, as you try your best to come to terms with it, but suffer so many losses of confidence that your stress levels (and cortisol) sky rockets.

Not to mention that being reminded by the mirror daily of the scale of damage to your breasts is a constant reminder that you have had cancer. If you are hoping to go flat *and* forget about cancer – you might be a little disappointed. My GP did point out that women who have had reconstructive surgeries also can't really forget they've cancer either – as those surgeries often result in multiple corrections and tidying over the years, also issues arise with implants too occasionally too.

Chapter 48
Managing Who You Tell What

I started to mega-manage my information to other people. This often meant keeping a lot of this crap to myself and my husband and saved other people from having to hear the broken record, and let's face it - they have enough of their own worries to go on with without me repeatedly misusing their time to trauma-dump.

The sad truth of it is that after your cancer has been chopped out and you are some way down the line - cancer is *to them* a distant memory – lots of people don't have the bandwidth to comprehend that far from you being 'fixed' or 'in the clear' – your life can feel 100% unrecognisable in the wake of the trauma that cancer brings.

Personally – I was doing a whole lot better in some ways when I was in the throes of euphoria about the cancer being chopped out in that first op, I felt positive about my future, I was completely naïve to the violent destruction to my legs that those innocent looking tablets that are aromatase inhibitors.

Another way of avoiding new stress is being aware when making new friends with someone, then discovering within seconds that they are quite happy to spill the beans on everyone else's private business is as sure way to get me running for the hills. I do not trust people who gossip, I used to gossip back in the 90's and always felt gross straight after so I cut it out. If they're talking about others, then they will talk about me.

My family's private information is not there as supply to sour windbags who've got nothing better to jaw about – I'd rather sit at home with my kids or brush my cat's hair or something – I'm just too old for this crap.

I developed a mildly ropey people-ometer which is 'if I went on holiday - would I trust this person to care for my beloved pet as well as I do' – if it's a 'hell no' – then it really is a 'hell no' and it all stops there. Sometimes it's a 'hell no' because I know they'd be nosing round my stuff, let alone how crap they'd be with my pets – if that's the case then it's a '<u>hell no' on steroids</u>.

Another people-ometer is watching how people treat waiting staff – if they treat them with the utmost respect then we are all good but treat them like skivvies and that's a beacon level red flag for me. I worked as a waitress for ten years and experienced whole new levels of rude.

Psychological stress WILL make pain <u>so much worse</u> – being brutal for your own sake, prioritising yourself – it must surely aid your own recovery and leave you in a better head space to support your own immediate family, children and pets.

I found that during and post-cancer – even to this day – I run on approximately 30% of the energy I had in all my years previously.

With your energy now being at critical levels – needing to guard it and nurture it with the same sensitive care you would give to give to a baby chick must surely help. Your ability to deal with other people's crap is likely to be much less – so being discerning about whether you really need to involve yourself in other people's drama and if you can step back do – due to cortisol (released in stress) - your life might literally be depending on it.

My sensitivity and hypervigilance to other people's unkindness magnified hugely post cancer – looking back, it feels like I became completely intolerant of meanness overnight.

Drawing in close – those people who rock up saying 'what can I do to help'. If you don't have any of those – at the very least – pushing back those who 'take away' from your life will help.

If you can, consider minimising time spent around people who push your buttons. They know what they are doing, and you do not have time for this.

As mentioned earlier - nobody has 'the right' to have information about you – being aware that your information is supply in the wrong hands and can come back to bite you when you least expect it can be helpful.

My ability to deal with assholes diminished in a steep step-like process with every surgery and new aromatase inhibitor. By the third op, and the fourth war with aromatase inhibitors I just decided that enough was enough.

My pain was not going to budge – so unnecessary drama had to go.

What are your supports like? – If we are unlucky, they can feel like an albatross.

I have also realised how pointless it is for me to listen to criticism from some random inner voice of my own, it doesn't help me at all – so I now verbally argue the toss with it and can be heard saying aloud 'actually no, I'm not rubbish or lazy today' – *'I've had a bad night and I'm doing well in spite of it'* I now try to say to myself if I notice it. No one can ever hear me do it as I'm fairly discreet – but I won't let my inner critic win anything these days.

Doing what we can to minimise the *inner voices* of other people can help. The people whose voices these are don't have to be anywhere near you – but you hear their voice in your mind like a nasty tapeworm that works its way round the corners of your mind when you least expect it.

Seeing if you can push them out to the periphery, turn the volume of their voices down, and if possible, detach from it might help. The less you give these people headspace in your life – the quieter their voices become and the more you increase activities that 'fill up' your cup and set you on a path to *become you* – the faster you can shut those pesky voices up.

I found watching some online videos on this very helpful, overall the consensus seemed to be around 'just because you have an outside person's critical voice in your head – doesn't mean to say you have to put the focus on it, just gently encourage your attention onto something else, without backing yourself into a corner and panicking about not being able to 'get rid of the voice'.

For those who have gone through traumatic childhoods – this critical voice may have been around for a long time and is not going to go without putting up a fight. We have enough to contend with as it is, without other people's crappy critiques of everything we do micromanaging our lives when they're not even there!

I've only just started learning about becoming your own cheerleader or parent – where you can develop another inner voice that argues the toss with your critical one, who has incredible common sense, is forgiving, could be for some the parenting you never had, and most of all has your back.

Chapter 49

Things I'd rather people didn't say to me...

- Wow – doesn't your tummy stick out without your boobs to balance you out!
- Are you pregnant?
- WHERE'S YOUR PROSTHESIS?
- Has your cancer come back? – you haven't got secondaries have you?
- So – you're cured then?
- You're gonna have to really reflect on what you did that caused this aren't you.
- Let me tell you about a special diet that cures cancer…
- Lucky you found your partner before you had your boobs chopped off eh!
- WHAT?! – you didn't take the free boob job/tummy tuck?
- Well – you've got pain but at least you're not dead – my neighbour's friend's daughter died last week – at least your still here.

- I think you're *ever* so brave to go out like that.

My final final word here – is that speaking from personal experience, when I'm going about my business, going to the supermarket, eating out, having days out – I'm not constantly thinking that I look a state or that I need to be worrying about what my lack of breasts looks like.

It's only when people start saying this crap that I remember my flat-ness. So although the way I look is different – believe it or not, my world doesn't end because of it. I just wish that people could think twice before letting this crap erupt from their mouths as it just isn't necessary to say this stuff. They clearly have a problem with my decision to go flat and feel like they need to tell me all about it. (I've given reasons for exactly why these comments are thoughtless throughout the book).

Other conversational options could include: –

- How are you?
- How are your family/pets/hobbies?
- Have you got any exciting plans?
- What can I help you with?
- Would you like to see some cool photos I took of…
- I love your necklace/dress/hair.

Anything – but this crap. Please.

This sounds very unkind – but when people are pointing out my different-ness in these ways – I am not pointing out their different-ness at all, I could say equally shocking things to *them* about *their* appearance – their choice of hairstyle, their figure, not to mention how I could appraise their personality faults or quite obviously their lack of tact – but I don't – I pop my filter on and keep it to myself. In truth – I'm not that interested in whether I think other people look terrible or not, because my focus is on my family and wellbeing instead. Rudeness traffic goes both ways, and it would be a better world if we just took a moment before we launched sometimes.

Chapter 50

Other Tips

Waitress aprons bought online

I read ages ago in an online group that waitress aprons are fab holders for wound drains. These were some of my best purchases. Mine had three slots in them, I was able to pop two drains in post mastectomy, which saved me carrying them by hand – which was a real nuisance.

Record the Nurses Wound Management Advice

Ask if you can video the nurses' instructions on discharge (you don't have to video the nurse's face, just point it at the floor and record her instructions). I was able to manage my own drains at home. I was quite dippy in hospital, so asked the discharging nurse if I could video her demonstrating how to empty my drains – she said yes, and when I was at home I was pleased to be able to do this, as I then didn't need to have health visitors in my house (bringing in bugs too – that I could well do without). I had to note down how much daily blood loss I had, which was very easy.

Splash out on some front opening nightdresses or an oversized stretchy nightie

That's for post op – the button up nighties are great for when you see the medic, you don't have to bare quite as much when they are inspecting the wounds.

Beyond that, I moved onto oversized stretchy nighties as they had more give in them when turning in bed.

Splash out on cotton nighties and vests for those hot flushes. I've already mentioned the cotton sheets underneath for hot times of year. The feeling of brushed cotton mid hot flush made me literally want to peel my skin off. My husband was so kind and bought me an electric blanket – I tried it once and nearly had a mental breakdown as it triggered a violent hot flush and then I couldn't escape from it. It was very sweet of him to buy it, but it did end up on his bed instead.

Get yourself some underwear that makes you feel good

I've mentioned already, about how much I love my plain cotton vests. For those who want to feel a bit fancier – there's a particular brand that makes some gorgeous sexy underwear especially for flatties – I haven't tried any of it yet – but I'm sure I will at some point.

Alternatively, for a while, I wore little supermarket bra tops which made me feel a bit more secure with my wounds covered. I usually just wear a vest now though.

Don't overthink what to take to hospital
I spent so long worrying about what to take for the first op, I wasted a lot of time researching it in online groups etc. By the second op I wasn't so worried, and by the third – I couldn't care less. I could have gone to the third op with a grannie's handbag and been delighted with a pair of tea coloured tights, half a pork pie and a bag of mints.

Take care of other aspects of your health if you can
I found that on 30% energy, managing severe disability and chronic pain – my capacity to deal with other run of the mill pain like a tooth falling to bits became increasingly difficult. A broken tooth is bad enough as it is – but it's just too much to deal with these extra bits on top of everything else.

For that reason, I recommend attending to personal care as much as possible.

If you're able to look after your teeth for example and prevent significant tooth pain (and expense!) – it will help you in the long run. I've always taken my chompers for granted, until recently when I foolishly thought I could still crunch boiled sweets. A molar disintegrated in my mouth causing a vile pain and expense that I could well have done without. I managed to wreck some of my teeth on a couple of occasions. If you're able to head off any of these problems by taking care of your beloved gnashers now – I would go for it.

My hair has thinned out
I'm not sure if this is due to the aromatase inhibitors or just post-menopause and thyroid issues – but whatever – I'll mention it anyway – and it's just to say that I'd become increasingly self-conscious about my lack of hair which was doing nothing to help my confidence when going out. I started to find a way of quickly styling my hair in a much softer, kind of way, with it in a loose bun at the back, and lots of fine tendrils coming down all around, especially around the fringe area – which does seem to help with framing my face in a much gentler way. I hadn't worn jewellery for years – but I have started to wear earrings and a pretty necklace and it does make me feel a bit prettier once I've put on some natural looking make-up too.

Ready meals/easy food
On discharge from all three operations – as mentioned earlier - I took it upon myself to swing by the petrol station which had a well-stocked mini mart selecting a plethora of ready meals. I did not want to kill my husband by 'death by carer' – he had enough on his plate cleaning four cats, two children, a house, way too much washing, let alone chef-fing up some sort of cordon bleu effort for me. So, I stocked up with as many ready meals as I could, some custard slices, egg tarts for protein and packets of baby rusks – which I craved in all my recoveries – must have been some sort of bizarre regression as also drink endless amounts of hot milk for comfort. (We don't usually have ready meals in the house though).

Don't eat raw cake mix prior to ops
I almost derailed one of my operations by getting the-mother-of-all-mega-trots after 'licking the bowl' on a rare occasion I made cakes. I don't recommend eating raw cake mix prior to a big op.

Be careful with knives pre-op
I regretted purchasing a razor sharp veg knife prior to my first op – the nurse eyed me with horror as my hands were covered in so many cuts – they were quite deep too, I had forgotten just how sharp new knives can be.

Be careful with your pets pre-op
My beloved cat scratched me pre op – the sore was a bit raised for a bit which didn't help my worries, skin infections pre-op might delay your op.

So many instances where I had a bug bite, an animal scratch, even a scratch from my lovely extendable back scratcher caused sores that struggled like hell to heal on their own. The bug and animal scratches took months to heal, in part because I had a couple of lymph nodes removed, in part – I'm guessing – because my body was healing from major surgeries too. The healing of these type of wounds did however speed up over time.

Hand over the pet cleaning for a couple of weeks post-op
I handed over cleaning the litter trays to my family for a couple of weeks. To save me flicking bits of cat turd into my flappy bandages.

Cheap as chips bath towels are great

For single use so that you're not drying your wounds with festering fungi. I found the thinnest bath towels, they were two quid each or something like that. I could use them once and chuck it in the wash. Better than smearing fecal bacteria that's festered in a warm room all over your open wounds the following day.

Sort your drawers out

I regretted not having gone through my drawers and wardrobe to remove stuff I rarely wear prior to a couple of the ops. Overstuffed drawers which do not glide in and out easily are going to jolt your chest wounds if you need to ram them shut. Such a simple thing, but after a double mastectomy – you'll be very chuffed if you can go straight to the items of clothes you want without a big struggle. You won't have as much strength in your arms, and if you do – you shouldn't be using it as you might disrupt the surgery under your skin – let alone your skin wounds.

Exercise is key

Sounds a bit standard and boring to some of us – I know it did to me before I got started exercising. I can't emphasise enough how key this was to managing my daily life better.

Post operations, lying around in my bed eating cake getting heavier and weaker annihilated my mobility for weeks once – it was almost like having to relearn how to walk again after one op.

Motivational videos of a particular person telling me to 'get the heck out of bed and work out' has helped me to create a daily exercise routine first thing after my coffee every single day. The cost I chose to take was removing the ads, so I can play these videos without a million ads driving me mad. I roll out my exercise mat, and do some simple leg, core, abs, and weights exercises. I have just one pair of hand weights and with just 20-25 minutes a day – my body is gradually transforming from one that was weak, wobbly and struggling to one of strength with vastly improved balance on the stairs. So many motivational videos – I was surprised at how quickly they can help when I wake up feeling sorry for myself, I pop one of those on, and many times I am able to change my frame of mind by using them.

Food considerations/healthier eating
I'm still having a nightmare with this.

I had got into a vicious cycle with eating – I would have a difficult day, add into that some incoming stress from an outsider and my sleep could be ruined. If my sleep was wrecked – there was a high chance I was going to stuff my face with toast and cake the following day – and so the cycle continued. It was beyond frustrating – particularly if incoming stress from an outsider was completely unnecessary.

Mobility wise – I'm doing a lot better eating low carb – though not the extreme version. I'm trying as much as I can to cook from scratch which is also saving money.

Some days it does all go down the toilet though, and I'm so tired or in pain that I end up eating junk food. Thankfully this isn't often these days, and I rarely hit the crisps, cake or chocolate and never hit the wine. If I do go wrong – rather than chastise myself - the next day, I forget about it, I don't berate myself, I just reset back to healthy food as far as possible and get on with it. Thinking about it – it's bread that is my downfall every time – but I am trying to be a lot more sensible with my consumption of it.

Only yesterday, in my bid to be healthy I ate almost a whole bag of spring greens, and at bedtime was shocked to be awoken by great big trumpety farts! How long have I been farting in my sleep? – my poor husband.

I have had such a nightmare with weight loss. I recently started to wonder whether I should try the new weight loss jab. Being post-menopausal, it seems that my fat stores are the next place that oestrogen is obtained from, so it makes sense to reduce my body fat. If my own fat is putting my health at risk, then maybe it's worth considering the weight loss jab. No one really wants to take medicines that haven't been around for years though, but I will give it a bit of thought, although at time of writing just prior to publishing – I'm not keen.

I had a go at eating super healthy for a bit, and I heard that creating my own gut-biome mix of nuts and seeds was a useful thing to have on the side in the kitchen in case you are peckish. My husband was not exactly on board with this at the best of times, but one day he took a mouthful of it and nearly broke his teeth. He came rushing in to announce that it tasted t e r r i b l e with piles of it falling out of his mouth. I said what have you eaten – 'butt-giome' he said in a state. It wasn't – it was the broth mix by the cooker. He says he doesn't recommend eating raw pulses – he was bad for a week.

Herbal tea
After my first op – I made a beeline for all things natural thinking this was a good thing. I did however discover that if I stopped drinking a particular herbal tea – my hot flushes significantly reduced – this is possibly a coincidence – but I took a rest from drinking it just in case. In the end I stopped all herbal tea in case it triggered hot flushes.

Added the day of publishing – this week, I reintroduced just normal builder's tea (black tea) and experienced the mother-of-all spate of hot flushes – gutted – just gutted – I can't have anything nice : (I will work around it but wow it is annoying.

Alcohol
I can't tell you what to do about this. Personally – I felt I deserved more than a few glasses of wine after being diagnosed with cancer, and I really enjoyed them too.

Long term though – it caused me a huge number of problems that eventually led to me binning it off. I couldn't balance the fun and relaxation of a few glasses of wine, with the next day being ruined due to my already low 30% energy being shattered by alcohol tiredness. Add in the 3am waking with panic attacks and subsequent anxiety throughout the following day – alcohol's card started to get marked a year or so ago, and my final decision to get rid of it has been one of the best decisions I've ever made.

I do miss it occasionally, but knowing it's one of the biggest factors for preventing a recurrence does not make me crack open a bottle. In time, like I say, I came to find a different drink for bedtime that felt like a treat – for me it is hot milk – not very exciting for most, but I look forward to a couple of mugs of it and it works for me.

Meditation
I discovered that a particular type of mantra meditation was leagues ahead of all other meditations for me personally – and I have tried a few types of meditation, including a years teaching course on a different one.

None of the others stood the test of time. With mantra meditation I can get to a light place of almost weightlessness which is blissful as it recharges me and helps with my pain.

It can make the difference about whether I'm desperate to lie down at 6pm instead of 1pm. I use this meditation daily and it has been by far the most useful.

Listening to things
Listening to a book, podcast or music – distraction can work in terms of some pain and mental health issues, not all granted, but it can be worth a try.

In the beginning, I used to pop my phone into an apron pocket, or my bum bag and listen to a good book. It made chopping veg and putting pants away so much more enjoyable. Eventually, I bought some earphones and haven't looked back, as they also drown out the racket of the washing machine -yay.

Planning for stressful days
You can manage daily life, but disruption like when your kids are ill can make your days hard, so if you have kids, having a spare duvet always available and a sick bowl permanently under their bed – it does help for those unexpected moments of sickness. A well-placed bowl can save hours of washing and scrubbing carpets too, something about a stitch in time there. Having as many systems in place to cope with adverse situations can take the stress out of what feels like a mini crisis.

I have spent the past three years also trying to head off unnecessary trips to the Emergency Department. This, I'll admit, has involved some helicoptering of the children to spot an accident before it happens, but it feels like it's worth it, as nobody wants to spend seven hours in the emergency department, especially if it's preventable.

It feels so selfish, but it's hard enough to go about the bare minimum of business on your bad days, if you throw into the mix a vomiting child, or a partner laid up with lurgy – then you're in for a real treat – a grindingly difficult few days where you feel dishearteningly behind with everything. And once they're better - you're on catch up with the washing, the bedding etc. Not easy at all. In the end, if we had a week like that, I just asked myself *what I could take off my to do list?* - maybe cooking from scratch was the first to go, and I could make use of simpler meals that came from the freezer and didn't need so much washing up on those hideously bad weeks.

Making New Mates can be Tricky when you feel like Crap
I repeatedly make a hash of making new friends, I look terrible, I'm tired, my patience is shot, I say the wrong thing, it's just not happening.

To top it off, with all the content around the psychology around *understanding the challenging and toxic people in our lives* – I find it impossible to 'unsee what I can now see'. It usually goes something like this…

1. I meet a new possible friend (usually a parent of my kid's mates), we put our best forward, chat a lot, smile a lot and get on really well a couple of times.

2. I then keep putting off meeting up again because I feel like crap, look sweaty and my clothes are from supermarkets and my shoes look like I dragged them out of a skip.

3. By the time I do meet them again, I'm so consumed that I've probably irritated them with my unpredictable energy, that I start acting weird and so do they.

4. We don't meet again.
Either that – or …

1. I meet a new person. It goes well for approximately 40 minutes. A few red flags later I realise it's a hideously bad fit and I never want to see them again.

2. I protect my peace and hang out with my cat instead.

3. They are pissed off and it's awkward when I bump into them in the bog roll section of the supermarket.

4. I get palpitations in the supermarket forever and wear earphones to drown out feeling overstimulated with panic about bumping into them again and saying something idiotic.

5. I start researching 'how to be a hermit' or I embark on research to see if they need people to look after the birds in St Kilda.

I say all of this, and have to wonder if It's me who's farting out enough toxic vibes to blow a Gieger-meter. I'm not gonna think about it.[6]

Supporting your nearest and dearest

I'm extremely lucky to have a fantastic husband who has supported me through every aspect of this journey. The mental and physical toll of my own trauma – *must* be difficult for him sometimes – he never says – but he does look tired. I try as much as I can to help him by helping myself, doing all the things as stated above to ensure I can care for my own needs as much as possible before asking him to help me.

I try to organise my day so that I am able to cook tea as much as possible. If there are nights when he drives the kids to after school clubs – well then those are the evenings when

---

[6] Actually, my OCD tells me *we are* going to be ruminating about the question - *Am I a Massive Narcissist?'* and examining all the evidence, as the topic for this month. Fantastic.

we will all have hot sausage rolls from the freezer for tea, or pizza, as on those nights we need minimal washing up, as no matter how well I manage my physical pain, there is an upper limit to the time of day I can continue standing for, and that ends at between 5pm and 6pm.

When my mobility is particularly bad – I try to cook from scratch early in the day. If we're having something like spaghetti bolognese for tea, I try to cook it in the morning, cool it in the freezer for an hour then put it in the fridge. I'm always grateful I've done this by tea-time because by then it just wouldn't have happened.

You might feel guilty
About the disruption to your family – especially the kids. It's a lot of to-and-fro with so many hospital appointments – it starts to feel like your surgeon is obsessed with you.

Until discharge where you'll be lucky to drum up interest from the cleaner when you call your breast team. (Bit extreme really, mine have been great lately, but on my off days it just feels like this x).

Taking responsibility
Trying to be aware of the vibes I'm putting out seems to help the general atmosphere of the house. I'm constantly checking myself, particularly if I haven't slept well and am grumpy.

Always being willing to apologise as quickly as possible hopefully reduces my kids future need for therapy, as does – just accepting that there are the occasional days when it's hard to see the bright side of anything, and knowing that I'm a misery guts, just taking my sorry-ass on up to my room and watching telly – far better than resentfully wafting bad vibes around the house like some kind of toxic incense that nobody wants. Bad moods cause a domino-affect in the house, and you <u>don't</u> want the whole ship going down.

They've also had a lot to put up with, and the least I can do is my best to nurture their morale and minimise the crap I put out into the house.

Fleece jumpers
Fleece jumpers are lovely for when you feel absolutely frozen, or just a bit sensitive on your breast area post op. I found myself being really fussy about what fabrics I wanted next to my skin for ages.

Cooking can be a nightmare
I had so many periods of time when my ability to cook tea was an absolute nightmare. I've mentioned peeling veg sitting down is helpful, but there are other issues relating to cooking too.

So much food has been wasted here, because I was stuck in a catch 22 situation – If I bought too much fresh food, I couldn't always predict how my energy would go, and on a really bad week we'd end up throwing much of it out as I just wasn't physically able to stand to cook it.

I started freezing fish and meat, but no sooner as it was defrosted in the fridge, I would have a bad day and that would get binned too. It was so disheartening when we were trying to save money. We've stopped buying too much fresh food now, it takes the pressure off having to cook something that seemed like a good idea on Monday, but by Thursday you feel like death. Having a few bits in the freezer has been better than nothing.

The shame of throwing out lots of food bought with the best intentions, owning (used) recipe books from all around the world, buying the entire spice selection to whip up Moroccan food complete with lemons in jars, and then just making the same food I always make makes me very disheartened. I enjoy cooking, and it's most upsetting to waft past my stack of cookbooks with a tray of pies from the freezer, but I have to try not to be so hard on myself, as it isn't every day, I try to cook from scratch as much as possible, and aromatase inhibitors will one day stop. Trying to fall back on foods that are quicker to make even if it is just scrambled eggs, mackerel, or beans on toast or a baked potato is about as good as it gets. When I am able to make a curry – I try to make twice as much and we have it the next night – not a new idea, but one that does work when I can do it. Another good one is buying a huge tray of drumsticks and putting a jerk style spice on them and then at least the family can grab them when they want (I buy the jerk style spice that comes in a tin – which will obviously not be anything like the real thing cooked from scratch – but when I'm exhausted this is a delicious substitute).

Mental health support

I avoided using NHS mental health services as a support for my mental health over this time. I got myself into the 'no one is coming' mentality and that suited me better.

If I had started to pursue help from the NHS, my fear is that I could have slipped into victim mentality – especially knowing how stretched their services are – I could well have received little quality or no support from them and become disappointed, which could end up with me feeling far worse.

I decided instead to look up therapy programmes online and invest in one of those – I could watch the therapist teaching sessions in my own time, and work through the exercises – this felt hugely empowering – to soldier on obtaining my own support without having to hustle to get it through our struggling NHS.

I <u>definitely don't</u> want some over-stretched with a high caseload, burnt out nurse, who's probably skipping her lunch break and dying for the loo to *have to* see me.

I can detect staff who are treating me like a customer at a cheap restaurant – *'get 'em in and get 'em out'* mentality is not conducive to me doing good therapeutic work – so the healing programme that I do under my own steam suits me much better – I'm steering the ship and I feel more in control.

I am extremely wary of handing my mental health over to a professional. No one can rescue me with even the speck of the power that I have over my own future – so I prefer to do it myself. That said, using additional support to complement the power a person has seems to make sense.[7]

Try to manage your energy

If the aromatase inhibitors are grinding me to a painful halt after lunch, then I try to make sure that I'm sat for at least thirty minutes, which seems to be enough respite for my legs to get moving again. Don't get me wrong, my legs will still be sore, but the rest just helps enough for me to get through the day.

Mantra meditation in the afternoon can lift me out of a terrible slump.

Consider playing around with the time of day you do housework etc.

Apologies to those who have physically challenging jobs, as this bit clearly won't work for you – you can't exactly rock up to work and say you'll only do the physical stuff in the morning. But for anyone who does get the chance to do physical stuff early in the day – I do recommend it. I work from home, and changing a bed in the morning means I get a fresh bed at bedtime, whereas if I left something like that to later in the day, the chance of me doing it is far lower – due to crap energy and stiffness.

---

[7] Obviously there are times when we have no choice but to take what support is offered – I just try to stave that off for as long as possible – and I totally understand that there are times that the best of us just cannot cope, and need a bit of help to get on our feet again.

You could experiment with what time of day you take your aromatase inhibitors.

Initially – I wasn't keen to take aromatase inhibitors at 7pm, I had read somewhere that it might keep me awake at night. Having said that, I got so fed up with taking it in the morning and gradually noticing my mobility becoming more stiff, that I thought a radical experiment was worth a go. I've gone from taking aromatase inhibitors at 10am to taking it at 7 or 8pm – sometimes I sleep better on it as the heaviness that used to come over me in the afternoon seems to come over me at night, although I have had the occasional wakeful anxious nights on it too. It seems to be a mixed bag at the moment – time will tell if I keep to taking it at night. Taking it at night has improved my mobility significantly in the day though, I feel like all the pain must hit me at night, and I'm resting, so I'm not aggravating it. Whereas previously, the side effects worsened as the day went on, in line with how active I needed to be at those times.

Supplements I take that make me feel like they are easing the aromatase inhibitor symptoms.

- Cheapest loratadine from budget supermarket – I have experimented with this, and there were occasions when my knee jammed up completely, and I took one of these and it freed it up again, still painful, but more movement and some reduction in pain. It doesn't always work, but I now take it daily in case it does.

- Cherry tart capsules. (I tried the juice but yuk it was too strong). I have no idea if these help with aromatase inhibitor symptoms but lots said they did and I thought it was worth a try.
- Sublingual vitamin B12 complex recommended by an influencer. No idea if these are helping symptoms of aromatase inhibitors or not.

I'm not recommending you take any of this, I can't give you any evidence for any of this being any use – but I mention it just in case it's something someone wants to look into it for themselves.

Radical Acceptance

I learned this term watching a psychologist online video. For these purposes, I take it to mean that I just need to radically accept the changes in my life, the adjustments that I have to make daily in order to live. Yes – life is tougher compared to what it was before, but there are also aspects of life where I am wiser – so It's not all bad.

Coping with the Emergency Department

There were a few occasions when I had to get checked out at the Emergency Department.

Despite looking a complete state post-surgery – I still had to hang around in the waiting room for seven hours. Life feels bad enough as it is when you have to present to the Emergency Department – add into that you've been mangled by major surgery, you're exhausted and psychologically drained of everything you've got – it's a bitter pill to swallow that you have to wait so long, in such a horrible environment, surrounded by people vomiting and worse.

A lung or chest pain post breast cancer is an entirely different experience – I'm now acutely aware that cancer could return any time, and even if cancer *doesn't* return, something else like a heart attack could come out of left field and knock me off my feet. For this reason – trips to the Emergency Department are far more worrying now than they used to be.

I remember feeling devastated to realise, that my sudden panic at the Emergency Department that *the pain in my lung could be lung cancer* wasn't treated as an emergency at all – it's an emergency to me, to my husband and children – it would be a catastrophe, but not to the Emergency Department. I just have to sit and wait for seven hours like everyone else, these days I felt more like cattle than a human.

Incidentally, when I was finally seen – the nurse was a tad confused without me having nipples as a guide as to where exactly to place my ECG stickers. At first, when I raised my top, she didn't see my long horizontal scars, and she said, 'Oh your surgery is really neat!', until I had to raise my top a bit higher and she saw the long pink scars. There was a mild wincey moment, but it was fine, she was only young, and quite sweet actually. How lovely would that be if my mastectomy scars had disappeared altogether – hey ho.

On discharge, I got chatting to an older lady in the foyer. From the nose up, she looked exactly like my beloved, but long deceased gran. It was a strange but wonderful moment chatting to her, like my gran had come back to say hello. Her kind face, the glint in her eyes and her manner completely threw me out of all time – by the time I said goodbye to her and stepped into the car as my husband pulled up – I was completely thrown. You can always count on the Emergency Department for mildly strange experiences to happen.

Finding your comforts
(I have repeated some of these as they are comfort, and deserve their own section)

Little things like hot water bottles under sore legs.

Fleecy old fashioned bed jacket that makes me feel toasty when my body is cold through to the bone.

My salt lamps that cast a warm glow around my bedroom.

My fluffy bed socks.

My gel pillows that rescue me from boiling point in the throngs of a hot flush.

My heated gilet that looks after my lower back when it is sore – I just pop a power bank into the pocket and plug it in.

My heated vibrating knee device which is marvelous.

A padded wrist-rest for typing – all these little comforts can make a huge difference to quality of life.

A clip-on light for reading in bed, we have two single beds pushed together which gives us a little valley in the middle of the beds to stuff a fluffy blanket, said gel pillows and all those middle of the night things that I would not want to get out of bed for.

Ooh, lovely stretchy welly socks from a supermarket were wonderful for my sore legs.

Your feet might change size, or you might want comfier footwear.

My feet went up a size after all this. Not only that, but my ability to tolerate uncomfortable footwear is now minimal. I started out trying some really comfy slippers, but in the end, I've just bought some proper gym shoes for around the house which have extra support – and they are working an absolute treat – pure delight to walk around the house in those – I don't know why I put up with cheap crappy slippers for so long now. My knees take far less of a hit wearing trainers rather than poor quality slippers.

Move your bedroom mirrors if you want to
After a couple of years of putting up with seeing myself in floor to ceiling wardrobe mirrors – we finally ripped them out and binned them. I accept being boobless, but that doesn't mean I want to see myself getting dressed every single day. I like to be in the mood for it when I look in the mirror, maybe wear nice underwear, or check progress after a few days of toning. Catching glimpses of myself when I didn't expect it was demoralising and grinding away at my self-esteem. Now, I still have mirrors, but they are placed

more strategically so I get to choose when I see myself naked (or not).

After chucking out our huge wardrobes with mirrors – it felt empowering to replace half the wall with a 2 metre wide desk for writing. Now, instead of feeling awful when I caught myself in the mirror, I feel good about myself – that I have given myself a space to learn and practice writing instead – something positive for the future rather than looking at something I dread.

One last thing to note, is that for some reason I hate writing at a desk and staring at a blank wall – it makes me feel claustrophobic – so my husband managed to attach a big telly to the wall – exactly where I would have preferred a window to be – and now, I get to play ambience videos on the screen of things like a window overlooking a field, or cosy cottage window, or apartment window in new York type thing – depending on my exact mood. It's a wonderful thing to have a 'window' to look out of when I am working, if you struggle with staring at an awful wall when trying to write – I highly recommend this telly window thing, it's made a world of difference to my productivity.

I live in hope that one day I might be able to have my desk at a real window, looking out over a field with chickens, birds and lovely sheep.

Adjustments
I've gone from prior to cancer being zippy, motivated and in generally good spirits – to now looking at my husband

and wondering how the heck I could ever manage without him.

This can't be 100% attractive for him, but he seems to take it all in his stride. I've never been one for DIY – but now, if something goes wrong – I'd be in quite a panic without him here to sort it out. It's daft, because I was single for many years and fiercely independent before meeting him, I'm guessing my confidence has taken a huge knock, coupled with physical disability and psychological trauma it's going to take a bit of time to feel more confident again.

Phlebotomy can be tricky
After having two lymph nodes out, I was not allowed to have my bloods taken on that arm anymore – which was unfortunate for me and the phlebotomist, as the affected arm had been my good arm. I have piddly pathetic veins in my right arm – so this can be a performance if the phlebotomist is neither skilled, nor even worse lacking in confidence. Nowadays – I just mention to whoever is doing it that *they may prefer* to use a butterfly needle – as others have had more success with this, so far this strategy is working well – hurrah.

After I had the two boobs chopped off – I wasn't allowed to have blood pressure taken on either side. Oh my word, having to have my blood pressure taken via my very sensitive ankles was not fun, it actually felt quite humiliating. Eventually when my surgeries healed up – I was able to have my BP taken normally again – a huge relief for me as I hate my legs being fiddled with let alone being squished.

Dressing up for the doctor
I've done my own bit of research with this one, and I find, that if I make the effort to dress more respectably and make sure my hair is neat – I tend to get a warmer response from doctors that I am meeting for the first time.

It is sad, but I believe perfectly possible – that some doctors just think they are better than the common patients, and if I rock up looking like I just fell out of bed – I have been more likely to be treated less favourably than if I'd smartened up.

We make quick judgements about people (guilty as charged), and with all the poop we've been through already, we can do <u>well without</u> being treated like an idiot at the doctor's office.

Take it or leave it, but it's an approach I use these days – to minimise the chance of being treated like dirt. Fortunately, as mentioned previously – most of the doctors I have seen along this journey have been fan-bloody-tastic, they really did go above and beyond what I could have hoped for, particularly my lovely surgeon who saved my life – it's a cliché – but I'm never far from remembering that she saved my life.

I feel lucky that I have a good GP surgery, who when necessary – see me the same day, and 99% of the time have the bedside manner and patience of saints.

But there are unfortunately those medics who believe they are better than us, and with one whiff of us being uneducated or daft, will dismiss our concerns as 'anxiety' and limit how far they look into them.

I've deliberated over what causes official people to treat me like poop and apparently, it's 'the minute I open my mouth' it all goes wrong from there. Brilliant.

Also, making a bullet point and very spare list of what you are worried about really does help – I know someone who writes a darn essay every time they go – and it's only going to irritate a GP who has minutes to get to the point.

So, my motto is look smart, don't fidget and definitely don't gabble - then I'm in with a fighting chance. Don't give them a single reason to palm you off as neurotic or daft – your life might depend on it.

My sleep was never the same again
Don't get me wrong – I still get many, many days of fab sleep, but far from the idea that my sleep would be normal once the pesky expander was out - I actually get days where my scars wake me up with shooting pains, even three years on, after all this time, I wake with the pains that hormone blockers give me, and the hot flushes, I wake at 3am with a whole new set of worries for my children and my future. Things are just never the same.

After three operations I'm sorry to report that sometimes I still feel that tight banding around my chest like I've worn my bra to bed. Some days it just seems to pull tighter than others. What was it I said about radical acceptance : /

I'm adding this prior to publishing – that now, since the aromatase inhibitor has settled into my system (now taking it at night) – my sleep has become heavier than ever and I am now miraculously only waking once a night for a wee – this is a huge change for me as my sleep has previously been shocking and I usually nip to the loo at least four times a night.

You might become more fierce
I feel like I have changed a lot.

Maybe I now feel more confident in becoming myself would be more accurate.

One thing that has really changed is my work ethic – I'm almost a workaholic now, which works out fine as I love writing, and it still fits in around my family with my children still able to be my number one priority. But somehow – I've managed to push anything that isn't related to my family's future away and focus on the work I need to do to bring in more money, and after what I've spent in my early cancer journey thank heavens for that. I'd love to contribute to the family coffers and hope that will be possible if I work hard enough.

Armpit hair might go a bit weird post op
Your armpit hair may never be the same. Mine grows sparsely and is now much lower down than it used to be. I rarely use deodorant – my body's decision to sweat or not

to sweat seems to vary greatly according to my hormones and I guess having been mangled by surgery. It's cheaper for deodorants and the fewer chemicals I'm rolling onto my skin the better.

Those who supported you, and those who think they supported you
I know I touched on this earlier – but wow there's a world of difference between the two.

This was a bit of a rude awakening, I mean I'd always had doubts – but it took no time at all to see people's true colours. Some people are unbelievably *still perfectly happy to see you suffer* by *their* actions – the cruelty of others became all the more painful, and for me was never to be forgotten. This awakening caused me to take drastic action to preserve both my sanity and my peace.

I understand the difference between those who are on your side but are unbelievably bogged down with busy lives, but there are some people who you may have had suspicions about previously – who will now step up and show who they really are.

Some friendships just fell off a cliff the minute I had cancer – good old cancer ghosting.

These people will not answer when you call to tell them you have cancer, they will provide a litany of excuses for why they 'can't speak now' – yet when it comes to hearing further bad news or the nitty gritty of terrible things – they are right there with a bucket of popcorn. I had some 'friends' like this – who I'd always had some niggling doubts about – and I can tell you that it didn't take long before they disappeared completely.

I was only interesting to them when bad things were happening to me, which of course made them feel better about themselves. Not for me thank you – so I dropped those friends as soon as this became clear that that was what was going on.

It's the sort of friend that drops some chocolate off but can't actually talk to you about anything that's actually going on. It makes me want to wave my hand in front of their face to see if there's anyone in there – it's like I don't know them, and they certainly don't know me as they aren't asking follow up questions about anything.

I flourish around people who bring out the best in each other, cheer on each other's achievements and check in to see if someone feels able to talk about their health issues before charging in. I found it so violating that some people feel so entitled to my personal information without checking if I felt comfortable to talk about it especially in front of other people that I may not know well.

For a while, all you seem to be doing is going for tests, having treatments and waiting for results which leaves you in a state of anxiety – or as I heard someone put it online – 'scanxiety'. I was fortunate that this period of time eventually passed, and I was able to have space to start to rebuild my life, albeit a very different feeling one.

Realising I'm not responsible for other people's mental health

Adults are responsible for their own mental health; it's not my job to make a particular person happy, and realising this went a long way to me being able to stand in my own power.

The removal of people who didn't have my back in my life vastly improved the quality of what is left in generous measures. The plusses of removing people who mess up your peace is very much the gift that keeps giving. The more I did this the easier it got; <u>the peace is addictive</u>.

The bereavement that these relationships were not what you thought they were is inevitable, but in the end I decided peace with a splash of guilt was far better for my cortisol levels than anger and resentment.

Having cancer felt like being handed a pair of magic glasses that gave perfect vision of all those disruptors of peace. I discovered that by closing the door to some people, to stop chasing others, meant that the door was able to be open to new people, or just gave you better quality time with the ones who are *on your team*.

When you've finally decluttered your peace trashers and sour windbags - you can gingerly open your door again, and hopefully you might just have a ray of sunshine pour in where once there was gloom.

You might end up managing your mental health pretty well in spite of the crap

People mistakenly think that a diagnosis of mental health problems means that you are 'mental all the time' – well we all are a bit crackers at times aren't we?

I still experience a huge amount of stigma the minute people realise I have a bipolar diagnosis, I've mostly given up mentioning it now, as I have been high-functioning for years, and what people don't realise is that episodes can vary hugely from person to person.

There are plenty of people working across all industries including GPs – who live with a bipolar diagnosis. If we are lucky, the meds and/or incredible self-management means that we can be just as productive and active as anyone else.

In terms of the plethora of changes to your life that cancer brings – I just wanted to say that no matter how bad things have got, I've still found it possible to move on in increments, to still move through life in a forwards motion feathering my cap when I can, and resting when I need to.

Just because the poop hit the fan, doesn't mean that your life has gone down the toilet. Who knows what gems are inside of you, it could turn out that you are far more capable of attacking life with great gusto post cancer. This fierce-ness could be just the catalyst for you making cracking changes that you have been putting off.

There's a world of stuff that worried me pre-cancer that wouldn't worry me at all now. A career change, or studying online, travel abroad, or just braving it and going dating – there's so many small and big changes we can make to our lives. Cancer has just let us know that life really is finite, so no better time to jot down a plan and get going. If you need to make drastic changes to start shaping your life into something that matches *who you are today,* then there's no better time.

I'm thinking that it can't surely matter how old we are, to learn new things, or discover new interests. I recently discovered that there is no upper age limit to apprenticeships, not saying that as we get older, we are desperate to work for a pittance – but an opportunity to learn a new trade could be a wonderful thing for some. It's good to hear more about people changing careers and going off to university again in their older years.

You can still get good stuff done even when you feel terrible.
Interestingly, I did some of my best work when I felt really poorly on my meds – I was my most productive. So, it's not all bad. Be prepared to surprise yourself at how amazing you can be even when you feel like crap – who knows what you are capable of when you feel better!

Equally though, to be fair, many of us are exhausted, so treading water and self-care is just as important for as long as it is needed.

You might want to say no to a few things
I felt so bad for making arrangements and then letting people down at the last minute – especially if they had made

extra food for us, that I went full radical acceptance and decided to ward off all future engagements until further notice.

My energy was completely unpredictable mainly due to aromatase inhibitors but also post-surgery too, and an attack of pain could hit my knee right out of leftfield – there were days that I got up with full gusto – ready to embrace the day ahead, only to crash at 1pm and have to lie down due to agonising pain or chronic overwhelming tiredness – it was not unusual feel like 3pm was 3am, I could barely keep my eyes open, which felt like some sort of nightmare to keep myself awake – if I start napping all over the place – it's going to make my sleep worse, which won't help anything.

So, saying no to a few things, and reclaiming power in as many places as you can, can free up your mental space to start considering how you do actually want to spend your time and shaping your future into something that feels right for you. If it feels right for you, then that might improve relations with your own close family, as you may feel better able to cope with the day to day.

We get caught up in hamster wheels feeling obligated to keep doing *the same things with and for the same people over and over again* without checking in with ourselves about whether this is actually working for us.

Not everyone will like it, part of the process seems to be about <u>sitting with the uncomfortable feeling</u> that saying no brings about.

Do you keep doing what you are doing and then on your death bed resent the heck out of these people or do you make a stand now and just stop – which will no doubt cause you to feel guilty?

Discovering in my fifties that I also no longer need to say white lies to protect other people's feelings. For all my life I've agonised over *letting people down gently*, but inadvertently confused expectations and made everything *so much worse*.

From this point on, If I don't want to do something I am going to thank them for the idea and then say that I don't wish to do it.

Realising all these years I could have just said no, and avoided many a tangled web of confusion was <u>very</u> liberating.

There are some really good videos online about 'saying no'.

Solitude
I relish solitude these days.

It is also the solitude which with a bit of self-reflection – that can bring about changes that give your life a peace which is different from life before cancer. I do have future cancer to worry about, but then if I think about it – I always did – except I didn't realise it. But at least now post cancer – I know who I am, what I want and what I definitely don't want – and that has been wonderfully liberating.

On difficult days

When the trauma feels fresh – falling back on old calming favourites can be a bit of a winner. I spent the last three years watching old reruns of familiar telly. Whatever floats your boat. For me, these well-worn series became the comfy slippers for my mind, just enough interesting to distract me from ruminating, not too complicated to get into, but quiet enough to nod off to. Sleep hygiene in our house is about falling asleep with the telly on, we cannot for the love of anything nod off to silence.

Ambience screens online are also brilliant for setting the tone to the room whilst you are reading or checking your phone. I vary mine according to my mood, there's log cabins, vintage living rooms, Caribbean islands – everything to match where you want to pretend you are and I love them.

Sometimes, if I'm honest, I just feel plain lonely, and this is going to be the time that the ruminating thoughts start to pitch up, if I'm very unlucky they could be there for the day.

To counteract this, I tend to have telly on in the background for most of the day – particularly in the kitchen. I have found two particular channels to be perfect for interrupting negative thoughts and incessant worrying. Those are:

1. Miranda Mills – her channel reviews vintage and classic books which is right up my street. Miranda hosts the channel with her lovely mum Donna, both of them are a very calming watch, just what I need when I'm feeling

panicky or down. I can have this channel chuntering away in the background all day, and it's very safe watching, nothing scary, just gentle chit-chat about comforting books that they've read over a slice of home-made cake and a cup of tea. I feel more pure just for watching this, it's kind, and nurturing and I'm very grateful for just how professionally well-done Miranda's channel is – her and her mum's attention to the presentation of the channel – including the gorgeous flowers they always have can cheer up my darkest of days.

2. Hannah Rickets – now Hannah is the one that I have running if I'm feeling like going out and about shopping, or for a spot of lunch, she is wonderfully upbeat, has a great energy, can natter till the cows come home. She is based in London, I love London – and she visits everything from market stalls to swanky departments stores. She does lots of café, restaurant and bakery reviews too – ooh she loves her 'baked goods' just as much as I do so it's a lovely watch.

There are times when I would love to go out with a mate for the day, but my energy and pain are so dreadful that I just can't manage it – so watching Hannah is the next best thing, and I am very grateful for the hard work she puts in to making her channel as good as it is.

Just because people treat you like a sick person doesn't mean you have to behave like one
Ugh. Some people just really struggle with seeing you anything other than being ill. I've distanced myself from serial offenders and been glad that I did.

I had to push out the people who kept questioning if I was resting enough, or tired all the time, or generally pushing me into the role of 'patient' all the time. I am not cancer, I had *cancer*, and now I don't. I am battling with side effects of aromatase inhibitors, but I do have a life outside of those too.

You might still get breast screening reminders
I did.

I rang screening clinic number from my letter, and asked them to remove me from the database. There was a bit of huffing and puffing about this as apparently my GP practice was supposed to do this, and apparently, I should be calling the GP surgery to cancel them myself, but she agreed to do it in the end. Her trying to say that it was something I should do was a bitter pill to swallow, as in the earlier days – calling people to announce something like this 'I don't need breast screening because I've lost both my breasts to cancer' can be an incredibly emotional thing to say, often ending in tears which is embarrassing. Her coldness felt like a kick in the pants.

I was also handed out leaflets about breast screening when I went for my smear test, even though I had *just* been chuntering along about tales of my breast cancer to the nurse who did it. I don't blame her, they have standard leaflets that are given to everyone, and I'm sure like many NHS staff, she was probably thinking more about the next ten things she *has to do* than the finer details of my life, let alone the contents of the standard pile of leaflets she has to hand out.

You might forget for moments that you don't need a bra
I still see bras in shops and think ooh that's a nice bra, then remember I don't need one.

Watch out that you aren't missing other routine health checks
I missed my cervical smear appointment by months, after being lost in the vortex of hormone blockers. I'd taped the letter to the wall by the calendar and forgotten to book it – eek! Easy to do when your head is full of all this stuff.

You might develop a new empathy for those about to depart
Ahh, lovely Doris. And in general, I feel a pang of sadness when I hear about or see someone who is about to depart. Prior to this I felt something, but it is different now, it's more a feeling of life stopping to appreciate the enormity of the fact this person has lived a life, but soon it is time to go – I think this is why I read so many authors from 200 years ago, I'm trying to keep their voices alive, to breath them into my writing.

Sometimes I think about death so much I feel like calling the grim reaper to pull up and take a seat. There are just times when I go all existential and start wondering what the point of everything is – not so much in a mega depressed way – more – what's the point because we will all be dead soon anyway – more a resigned thing than depressed. Sometimes I wonder what the point of it all is if I'm about to check out anyway.

Draw a line under it with a special occasion
You remember I mentioned that big posh event that I was able to get a ticket to for my 50th birthday. This was nothing to do with cancer, and everything to do with where I saw my future heading.

It was wonderful to be a grown-up with my own interests at an event where I could talk to like-minded people.

It really did serve well to draw some sort of line under the poop-show and mark out the direction my future was heading.

Is there an event or training course that lies somewhere in the future of where your interests lie?

Dipping our toes into our future life can feel wonderful. If it challenges and scares you a bit even better.

If you can afford it or have it as a gift – treating yourself to a membership to interesting places
We made the mistake of buying a pass to visit castles all over the UK. A wonderful opportunity to get fresh air and some well-needed exercise. I hadn't fully thought through whether this option was going to appeal to our children – and wow did I realise it was a mistake after hauling them around several castles with them wailing with boredom so loud you'd have thought they were being tortured – a fitting

noise for a castle, but the passes were a bad fit for us as a family, so we binned off the pass and all agreed on an animal farm park instead.

The farm park was much more suitable, all on the flat, so easy to get around, tons for the kids to do, which left my husband and I able to rest whilst they played on the equipment and gave us a bit of time to ourselves.

Even if we didn't have kids I would have appreciated the farm park, as being able to pet and feed a whole range of cute animals is a great way of getting out of the house, a bit of fresh air and all those lovely endorphins being released when seeing the animals. I'm aware of some free city farms in the UK, perhaps there is one that you might like near you.

We stayed in touch with some wonderful friends from our previous life, – we met halfway-ish between us and them one day – at a science centre in the Midlands.

We had a fabulous day – although it wasn't without some interesting moments. It was one of those ironic moments that we had all congregated of all places in front of a giant sculpture of a woman with her huge great boobies hanging loose – of course no one wanted to make a thing of it so we just stood there nattering until we could move on to the next 'piece'.

A different exhibit had 'heat seeking' cameras, displayed on huge screens – and there we could all stand and guffaw at how silly our bodies looked. Except my body showed two bloody great lines across my breasts where my healing scars were! – how embarrassing! – everyone peered at my front, I covered my 'tits' with my hands and legged it. None of it worried me really – it was quite funny :)

People probably aren't noticing your flatness as much as you think

There does come a point when there is a sea-change, and you realise that people aren't really noticing your royal flatness as much as you think they are. People seem to be (quite rightly) much more interested in what they are doing, so this became less of a concern as time went on. For me – it took me about six months to a year to realise that I didn't stick out like a beacon with my flat chest as much as I thought I did. The self-consciousness just gradually subsides with a bit of time.

It is a massive operation – don't think recovery will be quick

Your body will heal when it's good and ready. Three years on – I still get a range of pains out of the blue across my chest.

Over time these ease up, but it's not unusual at all to have months with little pain at all, and then all of a sudden, I'm getting shooting pains around one of my wounds.

Wacky nightmares

I still get the occasional health focused nightmare – something like a medic coming at me with a huge needle. These nightmares are vivid, and colour the next day's mood.

They, like many other aspects seem to become fewer over time.

I still cover my chest with embarrassment – particularly around the children
I still feel just as embarrassed about my naked frontage as I ever did when I had boobs.

It still feels very much like a private area, and my skin in patches can be just as sensitive as my old breast skin was. Another reason is that I don't want my children to worry about what I look like – my daughter showed signs of being worried about my scars too, so I tend to cover up on the run out of the bathroom.

Hats off to the women who raise money topless post mastectomy though – we are all different and how private we feel about our bodies remains a very personal choice, these women are raising awareness and saving lives, so I salute them.

Chapter 51

Final Thoughts

I now have a laser focus on my work goals and am now way further ahead with these since using those gaps in between the operations to study something towards this goal, however small. A few years in, and I'm starting to feel the benefits of this learning in spades, it all adds up.

There were so many times that I could have thrown in the towel, stayed in bed and bought a mobility scooter – (and I'm definitely not knocking people who need those) – the way I saw it, was that I was at a mobility crossroads – I witnessed first-hand quite how quick you can use your mobility – just one operation and a couple of weeks rest left me doddering down the stairs dangerously – I was at a much higher risk of falling, and it took months to regain strength.

I have a life to live with my beautiful family and the sooner I crack on with our goals the better, and part of this is working my butt off to study the subjects I love, which in the end don't feel like work anyway.

Some people seem to want me to rest incessantly, they can't understand why I would be hammering away at a keyboard and not sitting down all over the place - and then what? - later on get a crap job that I hate? – I've had years of that already; I've absolutely done my time with the crap jobs (I quite liked some of them but that's not the point).

You know that I don't recommend anyone get a flat closure mastectomy, because the years of physical and emotional pain are huge, but if you've read all of this and still feel that this is the right choice for you, then I hope at least one thing I've mentioned has been helpful to you.

Remember though that this is not the way to get any surgeon to agree to this procedure on the NHS. I only got my flat closure on the back of trying the chest expander for reconstruction and having a complete freak out, wanting it removed, and then just preferring <u>never to ever</u> wear prosthetics or knitted knockers.

The elephant in the room is that the chances of anyone getting this surgery on the NHS is as far as I understand it quite slim unless there are exceptional circumstances.

Flat closure mastectomy was definitely the right choice for me; I have no regrets.

Regrets and a drastic stress reduction strategy...
Regrets I have are not even close to worrying about my *lack of* wobbly front bits.

I have regrets about having given people such close access to my life for so long, when they are clearly not on my team.

Regrets about lost time to sullen, mean and controlling assholes over the years.

Regrets about career choices I made a mess of for so many decades.

Regrets about getting cancer in the first place – why did I have to drink and smoke so much in the past – did I half bang a nail in my own coffin? – I don't know.

I wish I could say to my younger self - 'If you are doing things now that are negatively affecting your health – I urge you to cast your eye to the future and how foolish you might feel when your parts are being poured over by a team of doctors, or you're having to be stuck in an MRI scanner because you *might have* given yourself cancer'.

I remember so clearly feeling like a real wally in the MRI scanner because I knew blooming well that there was a good chance I brought this on myself. In hindsight, smoking and alcohol are not so much fun when you've literally had to have your breasts severed off as a result.

How Ironic – that the little girl who grew up wanting *more than anything in the world* to be a mother, once becomes a mother – almost has the whole lot taken away, leaving her young children without a mum.

It's just terrible – so when I see that lovely glass of wine on the telly and wish I had one, I gently bring my mind back to why I want to live for as long as I can for my kids and go get myself a hot milk instead. Not suggesting you be as drastic as me when it comes to wine, but for me it was all or nothing and no in between. I'm sure lots of you could manage to be a lot more moderate with alcohol than I used to be.

Guarding my peace like a Doberman
It didn't take long before I realised that physical and mental pain squished my ability to tolerate mental pain coming in from the outside.

People are either helping me to protect my peace or trashing it. I binned a good portion of social media after it messed up my peace on nearly every occasion that I looked at it.

In the end there was no gain about looking at this crap, what was I doing scrolling through posts engineered to grab my attention and getting hooked into debating nonsensical issues online – it had to go and good riddance.

Discovering that some people seem really happy to talk to you as long as you are not doing any better than they are was a bit of a revelation. I avoid those now too.

There are some people who still wait for your fall despite them knowing that the fall would harm your children – quite bizarre, and it doesn't feel good to me.

These days my phone is now permanently on 'do not disturb'. I know, after all I said about wanting actual phone conversations – I do have those, but they're mildly planned first via text.

I read books, I listen to books, I talk to my children, I watch old movies, and I enjoy cuddling and brushing my beloved cats. Back to good old 1980's level of entertainments, and that suits me fine. I do watch the online app with educational videos though.

Negative people can get attached to you, it's difficult to get them unstuck. If you are able to ward off negative

Nancies and people who give you the heebie jeebies from the get-go, this will save you a lot of hassle and excess cortisol production down the line. See if you can get out early and save yourself.

Notice the red flags – if someone feels like a walking tragi-docuseries (and never ever seem to do anything to help themselves) – there may be times you need to give them a wide berth in case they trash your peace when you're feeling fragile.

In the age of social media where we now all know what everyone is really thinking – it massively triggers my hypervigilance, it can feel like I've got an audience permanently in situ criticising every single move – I honestly can't do right from wrong. How about I focus on my business and they focus on theirs.

Sometimes my peace has simply come from sharing far less about my business in the first place – less can go wrong if your news is under wraps.

I'm even more protective of my 'self' if I'm aware that particular people engage in 'mobbing' behaviours – that group backstabbing of others, that takes place often behind closed doors. A group of people lay into someone else for all the 'bad choices' they make under the guise of 'concern'. It is _not_ concern – it is just pummeling the poop out of others to make yourself feel better about your own life and I want nothing to do with it.

Other people I can't abide are people who are completely unable to have introspection about the things they do that harm others – these people NEVER apologise to anyone.

Two and a half years post-cancer was a big STUFF IT gear shift. One of my biggest takeaways was to stop chasing what is *not* for me.

Why am I chasing friendships where it's so one-sided – I don't feel I have this sort of time anymore.

By valuing my time and stop wasting it doing this it frees me up to focus on projects that <u>really do</u> serve our family, and it leaves more space for the people who really are there for me.

If you didn't feel invisible before – you may now.

I touched on this earlier, now that I'm getting older, I was already starting to notice my invisibility prior to cancer, without my breasts and now walking with a limp – for some I'm now completely invisible in public space.

I guess if I smartened up and dressed a bit snappier that this wouldn't be the case – but I'm not about to start doing that just to go to the supermarket.

The person I am on the outside looks nothing like the person I feel I am on the inside, and it's heartbreaking.

On the outside I'm that portly lady perusing granny pants in the market, but at home I'm busting moves to drum and bass in the kitchen.

I once told someone I'd still love to go to an old skool rave and the smirk on their face said it all. I might not be able to wear hot pants anymore, but I will get to that rave no matter what. What I wouldn't give to stand at the front and feel that bass again.

People will continue to say stupid stuff to you
Being told firmly by a lady at a car boot sale this week that *'at least I am alive'*, as her friend's daughter is dead after I dared to complain about the life of pain I have post cancer. This is just insensitive and actually a bit mean. Like I need to be shamed for complaining – thanks.

So, I'm supposed to just suck it up, shut the heck up and be grateful then – cheers. Interestingly – I'm always more shocked to hear mean-ness when it comes straight out the mouths of people who look really kind – you just don't see it coming.

Another person said that 'I ought to make a bit of effort with my appearance – you know – for my husband'. What a flaming cheek! – I feel like I've been dragged through a hedge backwards… yet if I'd have pointed out how rude this was, I would have come off the bad one.

Another hinted I should lose some weight, as it would help my mobility – gosh, I hadn't thought of that – thanks.

Added two weeks prior to publishing – the latest crap things a person said to me with great puzzlement was a startling - 'WHERE'S YOUR PROSTHESIS?', followed by 'See – this is what happens when you don't have boobs – your tummy sticks out', and then finished with ' 'I got to say it – I think you're ever so brave to go out like that'. Wow – just WOW – a spectacular triple-whammy of insults. And what the eff is there to be 'brave about' – is it that worrying for other people for me to nip out to buy a cucumber and dare to bare my flat frontage? I just struggle to see what the worry is. What *does or doesn't* stick out of my chest is no-one's business but my own – I'm not brave – I'm just buying veg. I think I mentioned this earlier – but if you decide to venture to the flat-side – be VERY prepared to have your personal appearance picked over, and as I mentioned just now - don't be fooled by people who look really kind – sometimes the cruelist words fly straight out of their mouths and hit you like a baseball bat – they then smile inanely and go on with their merry lives leaving you in a state of shock. How am I supposed to want to hang around with people that talk like this. They clearly don't extend the same courtesy of applying some sort of filter to their garbage so why should I spend time idiot-whispering them about why what they just said was massively offensive. Honestly – no wonder I'm a partial hermit these days.

Your bank balance might take a hit
As mentioned previously – for me – cancer was expensive, and people are not always understanding about how trauma affects different people in different ways.

Plate spinning
There are some days when I can't imagine being able to keep as many plates spinning as I used to in the pre-cancer days, some even when I feel like an absolute car crash of a human being. But then there are others when I'm like bloody wonder woman and I wonder how I did it – in spite of the painful legs and stinky sweats.

My life is <u>not</u> the same, but then I'm far fiercer now than I ever was, and my drive to get things done in spite of this poop-show is much stronger.

I do get days when I'm frustrated and exasperated that my body doesn't work properly – but I also get days when I'm zooming ahead with personal development far faster than I ever was before. Some days when I'm hobbling about – I wonder if it's all downhill from here – other days I think the sky's the limit.

I hope that your partner or supporters are kind
This journey is hard enough without anyone else making it more difficult for us. When it goes well – people are uplifting, encouraging and our best cheerleaders, but when it goes wrong they can hold us back and generally make every single thing we do feel an uphill battle. There are certain people that if I spend enough time around them – are quite happy to encourage me to question my own sanity – I absolutely do not need these people in my life.

Sometimes it turns out – that our best support is simply going to come from our beloved cat, or loyal dog, a comical parakeet, or even a herd of guinea pigs that serve as a wonderful distraction, or maybe the walk through the woods and feeding the beautiful crows who remember and come to rely on us as they loyally swoop down to see us. Don't get me started on how much I love crows – there are some fab documentaries online – and yes, they remember your kindness for years – they will swoop down to see you as they see your car approach. If you're going to feed them it's worth checking from wildlife rehabbers what to give them as they suffer with terrible health problems if they eat junk – there are some great crow groups online too – you might be astounded at just how many fans crows have these days since we've realised how intelligent, funny and at times very naughty they are! (Obviously crows cannot be pets, and those that are living in homes are usually because they are disabled and unreleasable).

It is hard on your loved ones – even your pets
No matter how resilient you are, cancer will affect your family in terms of massive stress, plus the disruptions to routine, hospital appointments, your recovery means that the housework may fall to other people because you can't do as much, to make things more tricky – cooking can be hard when you don't feel well, are tired, or in pain.

Try to be the protagonist in your own life
I don't know who originally said this, but I love it. I imagine I'm the lead character in a film, and I've hit those all too predictable difficult times three quarters of the way through – how will my movie end, I like to think about this and influence it in the best possible way.

I asked my writing mentor about whether I was too old to become a writer – her answer was – 'well you're not dead yet' and I thought *how true*.

It's not all rosy out this end – but I am wiser

Sadly, a piece of me died when I realised that all my life, I'd gaslit myself, that some people were nicer than they actually are.

Certain friendships that I had, had almost been 'all in my head' – I hadn't seen them for what they really were, I kept adding my positive spin on it, but I realised that the positivity was all coming from me – I was projecting onto them than they were far nicer than they actually were, and behind my back they were mobbing and backstabbing. I know they do this because they do it about everyone else, and unfortunately, I overheard things I wasn't meant to hear on numerous occasions which confirmed this. They criticised every single thing I do and I'm tired of it. I almost feel a bit thick to have realised this so late. It's like it hit me all at once that I have tolerated shocking behaviour all my life and never stood up for myself.

There have been plenty of people on my journey who refused to believe that I was even writing a book, or that if they did – they didn't think it would be any good. You know, those people who say 'she'll never finish it' or 'it's a vanity project' etc. – honestly it breaks my heart to think how cruel people can be, and people who claim to be on your side too.

How sad that it took cancer to realise that I have, all my life been at times complete pushover with these, when I realised – I felt gutted at the loss of time.

It's so sad too that it took me over fifty years to now feel like I've got a good measure of what life is about, I'm savvy, and grateful, yet fierce enough to be a real go getter for the later chapters of my life, yet how rubbish is that that all this wisdom arrives when it's no longer a given that you will remain in good health.

At this point, my goal is to protect my cortisol levels like a newborn baby. One squirt of cortisol and I'm gonna hunt down what the heck triggered it and take radical action to remove it. If I'm filling my face with cake after hanging out with certain people – then that needs looking at as the cake is now a threat to my life (weight gain = bad for estrogen cancer).

I can no longer have certain people anywhere near me. If it's between rude, and solitude, the latter wins <u>every single time</u>.

If my mean person detector goes off - then I'm done that very instant.

I am intermittently shamed for refusing to hang out with gossips and busy-bodies – they don't like me because I call them out when they are being unkind about a mutual friend behind their back. But when I point it out – I'm the bad one. And then none of them want to hang out with me because it's awkward. I manage to then get ghosted by the person I was sticking up for too, something to do with triangulation – it does my head in but for goodness sake I can't have mean people anywhere near me these days – I mean what is the point.

If I have to, I will just say – *'I can't do this today'* and go home.

If people spent more time considering 'why we don't want to hang out with them' they might be able to avoid us *running for the hills* when we just can't take any more.

I'm not some kind of sea sponge to absorb people's icky-crap.

Neither am I a sitting duck to be whacked when someone who can't manage themselves feels dysregulated. If someone is vibing with me all the wrong ways they can go vibe themselves into a cupboard and do that crap on their own. In fact, if someone is doing this crap to you on a regular basis, it makes you wonder why you keep them so close – giving them quite so much access to your life.

Too long, people have farted out their micro-aggressions at us, and we've been wasting energy pondering whether they meant it or not. – Yes, they probably did mean it, 'cos if you felt that barb pierce your skin then <u>yes they did send it, and yes they knew exactly what they're doing</u> – does this sound like someone who has your back? – nope – it sounds like someone just kicked your back to me. Are they on your team or not. I'm not saying I'm perfect – far from it, but from this point on I'm minding my own business and I refuse to engage in this rubbish.

Don't even get me started on emotional blackmail – this is just abuse.

Hearing people's most innermost thoughts on a whole range of crap on social media makes me want to live in a cave. Wow do I long for the 1990's when I was clueless as to what people thought, but it's too late now, the stable door's open and the horse has bolted - there will be no catching that one again.

All I can do is focus on building relationships with actual people, that I actually speak to and see in person. In recent years, I'll be honest, I've switched out a lot of humans for dead ones. I just read old classic books and pretend I'm hanging out with the author – they don't throw out barbs, act weird or cause me to ruminate for a week that I said something stupid. I did a lot of people-ing in the 1990's – I feel like I've done enough of that.

I won't bang on too much about this crap, but I just wanted to share some of the psychological ways that cancer has affected me.

I think, that as long going forward, my North Star is my children, my husband, my cats and my gorgeous friends (you know who you are you handful of gorgeous lovelies xxx) then I have a chance at making the next chapters of my life brilliant one.

The few mates I do have feel like I found them in the luxury-end-friend shop, not luxury as in posh, I mean luxury as in ultra-high-quality humans.

Oh wow – the relief and safety of spending time with people that are safe for me to let my guard down with, I can be vulnerable without worry, and they don't judge – mainly because each of them is busy enough managing their own varied and interesting lives that they don't seem to feel the need (or have the time) to judge what I'm doing. They don't need to beat me with a stick in order to feel better about their own lives.

These are the people who aren't 'suddenly silent' for my mini-wins, they are vocal and excited, and they encourage my growth as a human in this world.

They don't want to stamp on me, tell me where I'm going wrong from an ivory tower, or chuck out toxic barbs when they are having a bad day.

How I treasure these people, they are my chosen family, and I will know them for life.

Realising that Sometimes it's me Farting out Micro-Aggressions too

When I cast my mind back – there are some hurts that people have done that I just can't get over. I wish I could. And we are going back decades with these. I've tried to discuss with them, I've tried to forgive – but no matter what I do, I cannot take away the deep hurt that their words has caused. For that reason – I have to admit defeat in that whenever I am around them – I am very sure that I am farting out the odd micro-aggression here and there too.

Leaked feelings seeping out all over the place that the minute I mop them up – seem to spring out from somewhere else. If these hurts can't be fixed in the near future – then I think it's only fair to that person, that I limit how much I am around them. There is a good chance that they have suppressed all knowledge of saying *that thing* to me many moons ago, and if they do remember they will not believe themselves to be at fault – and so they could meet up with me in the current day, and be hit with wafts of irritation by this trauma of mine which is not anywhere close to being resolved.

These days – I just wonder what is the point of spending much time with people who I feel bad around, and then *I make them feel bad too*.

Unfortunately, therapy has helped to some extent – but in other ways the therapist confirmed their own horror at the hurt these people did which only served to deepen my anger. I'm so aware of time post cancer – and I don't have this sort of time to spend years in therapy trying to make other people's shocking lack of empathy and judgement feel in any way right. Therefore, some issues and people have had to be parked somewhat in favour of me focusing on what matters to me so much – which is my husband and my children.

(I have tried to discuss these issues with various people – but the outcome was so dire that if anything, it made the trauma more painful).

Saying Sorry
Another add on here (mostly with reference to my husband and kids) – is that something I try to do much better than I ever did – was that if I made a mistake – and did something that caused other people to feel bad, if it was my bad - I will try to own it.

Pre-cancer – I might have in a millisecond deflected ownership of the bad thing I did – and looking back I wonder what for. For example, something *didn't happen* over the weekend that *should have happened* and everyone in the house *might have* felt bad about it – but when I traced it back, it's because it's *usually me* who reminds people to do this 'thing' and I forgot to do it – hence it's *my bad* because I didn't remind anyone.

We had a chat, and from here on we are *all* going to check that this thing is done every weekend – so it is now not all on me. It's unpleasant to take responsibility for my own mistakes – but sometimes – in the grand scheme of things I have to wonder why it is so difficult. What on earth are we trying to protect – am I that fragile that I can't own mistakes – surely not. It's a work in progress – but I have been astonished at quite how many things do actually lead back to me when I really think about it, and hopefully me working on this might help to reduce other people's stress just a bit.

The Family Journal
On a lighter note, I've added this bit on just prior to publishing – I keep a 'family journal' – I buy the prettiest A4 notebook that I can find – usually one which has an image on the front that speaks to me at that moment in time – and just here and there log in it small and larger recollections of things that the family do.

It's not uncommon for me to forget to write in it for weeks, but I never berate myself, I just power on and add bits when I remember. A bit like when I'm trying to eat healthy – if I have one bad day I don't spend the whole rest of the year chastising myself for having one bad day – I just draw a line under it and keep going – who cares if there is a week or even a month missing here and there – it really won't make that much difference in the long run.

It can be just a simple line here and there, or sometimes it can be a three-page bonanza if we did something cool. I try to think ahead at what might actually be interesting to look at in future – like funny things the family said, an outing where something unexpected happened, or sometimes it's just mentions of the foods that the kids are obsessed with and even recipes of their favourites so they know how mum cooked them in future. I jot down what we typically eat for tea at that time too – not often, but it is in there somewhere.

I will admit that there is a part of me here which is jotting recipes in in case anything happens to me – which is silly really – but I like doing it and it gives me peace of mind that some of the things that are in my head are also in a book just to be on the safe side. The world wouldn't end if the kids didn't know how I cooked our Spag Bol – highly likely they'd be able to create a better one of their own - but it makes me happy and it doesn't take long so I go ahead and do it anyway.

Sometimes I attach tickets or the odd visitor leaflet of somewhere we've been, or a sweet wrapper of something unusual the kids tried (like some gross tasting novelty sweets they tried on a day out once). I even attach the odd note that my husband leaves for me, or a shopping list, and very occasionally a supermarket shop receipt – so that in future they could compare prices if they wanted to.

When I was first diagnosed with cancer – my first thought went to creating the memory boxes for the kids, and letters to them, and even a whole book dedicated to them from mum, but as my treatment went along and I seemed to not need to do this – but I still felt as if I wanted to do *something*. I had been keeping a family journal for a long time anyway, so instead of the memory box I just decided to put a little more thought into what I put into our journal instead. We now have a small pile of them, and I hope in future our children will enjoy flicking through them – or even showing them to their own children.

An add on to this – is that there are so many things that our family do that are ridiculous, and we fall about laughing, that we are about to start writing in an A5 book which we will name the 'Trauma Book' – it is will be purely written in jest – where we can all add a line here and there about something that *traumatised* them – usually like daddy singing such and such old fashioned song when they were trying to eat their breakfast, mummy's bedtime stories – (usually ropey anecdotes about bums and farts), or just anything that resulted in us all roaring with laughter at the dinner table because it was so terrible. We've joked so many times about 'putting it in the book of trauma' – that we will now actually create one and hopefully it will be a fantastic resource for creating some wedding speeches for the children in years to come. (There won't be any actual trauma in this book – it's just for <u>funny things</u> that happened).

(I didn't invent the idea of the trauma book or anything – just mentioning that we thought it was funny and will start writing one).

Chapter 52
Final Message To Reader

Well, here we are at the end of the book – I was listening to a book vlogger yesterday, chatting about an author who writes 'wonderful whimsical mystical tales' – and I thought oh dear - here I am with my first book about trumpety-farts and fat splash.

I hope I didn't come across to grumpy in parts – it's still early days, and I'm a bit like a dog that's just had three operations – I'm still tender and occasionally a bit snappy. Hopefully that will calm down as the years go by. Perhaps I'll read this when I'm older and wish I'd written it differently – who knows, but it is a snapshot in time, it has captured how I feel three years into gruelling breast cancer treatment and I've put it out there to help anyone who can relate. Overall, I still can't help but feel that I am never far from a precarious situation – hopefully that feeling will ease off in time. But you can see how I have come to feel on guard in terms of every aspect of my life.

I had some final thoughts about life and our choices and how much they affect us, that I wish I could have asked my younger self – I guess because now more than ever, I truly *feel* how finite life is, and how *before cancer* – I kind of wafted along in a bit of a daze at times not really realising that I had power to change the parts of my life that weren't working all along.

I'll share them with you in case any resonate – but please skip on if none of them do…

Have you chosen a profession you now can't stand – surely, it's not too late to retrain for something else – life is too short for you to spend it dreading your job.

Are you relying on your boss to notice how talented you are? – I used to do this, and it took me ages to realise that they are unlikely to notice at all, and if they do, they aren't going to tell you about it because they won't want you to leave, and if you're really unlucky they might be threatened by how good you are. If you are working in a crap job and hate it, and other staff treat you terribly, would you consider learning other skills so that you can exit this job at some point in the future. If you hatch a plan, and start now, who knows where you'll be in five or ten years, or maybe sooner.

Have you made decisions that you are now regretting – a job that turns out you hate, or you've moved somewhere, and you regret it – can you change it? This has been a journey of realising that at least we have a go at doing things, sometimes they pay off, sometimes it's a fat fail, but surely, we can fix this, we just need is a cunning plan and get ourselves out of it.

Could introducing some hobbies spruce things up a bit – focusing on one or two new interests and taking your time to learn them incrementally can massively build your self-esteem. Being just that bit pushy about incorporating your interests into your life can pay off.

Have you thought about writing your own memoir?

I make a hash out of plenty of things, particularly when I'm still learning – but we weren't born with this knowledge, so it makes sense that in the beginning we'll muff things up a bit – I'm not sure it's the end of the world if we make mistakes along the way.

Are you surrounded by people who are teasing you for trying new things – from where I'm standing, someone who braves it to learn a new skill – whether it be anything from going back to learn basic literacy skills because your school was crap, to retraining at 50, or doing a degree – all of it is progress, and has to be worth a go – especially if it builds our confidence and self-esteem. I still can't swim properly and fully intend to address this at some point.

If you're having a bad day – is there anything you can take off your to-do list so you can get to rest sooner. I'm home a lot, and I find putting old comfort telly on in the background, or book vloggers, or cute ambience screens that I like changes the record a bit in my mind rather than ruminating all day.

Wherever you are in this journey, whether you are the patient, the carer or just a random who's picked this up, just please look after yourself as best you can.

My body is falling to bits, and I regret the countless shocking choices that have littered my life. Maybe there's still time for you to save some of your bits dropping off like mine did.

The bottom line that I leave you with is that in truth - I neither recommend or not recommend flat-closure mastectomy. I had it, and I don't regret it – but I purposely sit on the fence about it, choosing instead to share how it was for me and then let you go about your business making the best choices for you. I know I said earlier that I don't recommend it – I recommend you don't get cancer in the first place – but for many of us we already got the cancer – so I guess I'm just saying that my final stance is that I sit on the fence.

Overall, my experience has been that once the cancer was chopped out, the struggle has been those darn aromatase inhibitors. I'm three years through that five-year long tunnel of these crappy meds, but it's worth remembering that for loads of us – there really is a life out the other side.

Obviously, we are making the best of our lives now too, but it's worth remembering that so many people have come through this, I've met some of them, in their 80's and beyond (obviously Doris made it into her 90's). One woman in her 80's served me in a charity shop once, she had had the same surgery at my age, and to her - like hopefully it will be for us, cancer was just one chapter in her long and fulfilling life – it had become almost a distant memory.

And all this panicking I've had about a recurrence – is real, but worth remembering that so many people who do go on to have a recurrence are living proof that there are treatments, and it's possible to live a full life for a very long time in spite of it.

My hope is that some of this might help some of you, and if it did then my mission will be complete.

I wish for you to be well, but if you don't feel well, I hope you will be better soon or can at least get comfy with some treats and generous amounts of love from family.

May your onward journey be filled with love and comfort, and for those who love pets – surrounded by your gorgeous pet family too.

Kate x

P.S.

Any mention of me enjoying my prescription meds – has been purely incidental seeing as I needed to take them for pain. I just re-read a bit where I said I was 'off my face on morphine' – well that would have only been the prescribed dose, I can assure anyone worried that I never even finished the bottle, and it is still gathering dust at the back of my kitchen cupboard. I am not an addict or anything like it. I don't drink, smoke or do drugs – just to reassure anyone who scan read the book and got worried – hot milk and the occasional bar of chocolate are my go-to treats – and that's as risky as it gets these days – I joke about the meds to give you a chuckle.

If you're thinking of taking pain meds *prior to* painful investigations – please check with your health clinic first, in case the meds might interact with meds they give you as part of your procedure, it could result in your procedure being cancelled if you are off your face on arrival.

I've mentioned throughout the book that I rarely use social media. I don't have any active (in terms of me posting anything) social media accounts – so in the unlikely event someone pops up with a social media account claiming to me – please look after yourself – because it won't *be* me.

I live with a diagnosis of bipolar, and whilst my mental health has been (all bar rocky moments) 'stable' for many years – I can't face doing the whole meet and greet thing, online chats, and other stuff which other brave authors do to market their books. Everyone is different – but for me –

a bad day on social media can be catastrophic for my mental health, so I have to politely bow out, and not partake.

My main focus is staying mentally and physically as well as I can, for as long as I can for my beautiful children and wonderful husband, so I hope you will forgive me for being quiet. I just want to play with my kids, fuss the cats and watch 1980's telly with my husband.

I am <u>here in spirit</u> - willing <u>you</u> - with all my might to do well, and I can't thank you enough for your precious precious time. Xxx

Printed in Dunstable, United Kingdom